KEEPING MY

BALANCE

A MEMOIR OF DISABILITY

AND DETERMINATION

By STEPHANIE TORRENO

Names have been changed to protect the identities of certain individuals.

ISBN: 978-0-9860388-6-0
ISBN 10: 0-9860388-6-5

Contents

To Mom
With Love

"Nothing in this world can take the place of persistence. Talent will not; nothing is more common than unsuccessful people with talent. Genius will not; unrewarded genius is almost a proverb. Education will not; the world is full of educated derelicts. Persistence and determination alone are omnipotent."
- Calvin Coolidge

Prologue

Mom and I always spent Saturdays together. Having lunch and going shopping, or seeing one of the latest movies, usually with Nana Adele and my sister Cris, started when I was a little girl. We continued this tradition through my teens. Even as I became an adult and Mom and I shared a townhouse, Saturdays felt different. The first day of the weekend became our time to have fun – just the two of us. In college, I knew Mom would convince me to drop the books, remove myself from the computer, and leave my homework behind for a few hours. These outings were our favorite time with each other.

I still see Mom on Saturdays, but our time together is different now.

My morning begins when my radio wakes me. The bedroom feels strange, yet familiar. Looking around the butter-colored walls, I remember the pictures and the mirror that used to hang on them. The bedroom seems sparse with my twin bed and light wood furniture, compared to the queen-sized bed and larger furniture that occupied more space. I picture the occasional mornings I used to bolt in the door to greet Mom. Lily, her Bichon Frise, growled at me to protect her territory if I attempted to climb up on the other side of the bed. Now, the room is my territory. In fact, the entire townhouse has been mine for almost a year. Only me, in a two bedroom townhouse.

I dress myself, apply my make-up, and make sure I have everything I need before heading downstairs. As I walk through the tiny hallway, I glimpse one of the pale pink walls in my old bedroom. If I have a few minutes, I may go into the office/guest bedroom and check my email or read the headlines online. Half the room sits empty without my daybed or other furniture. My cousin Laurie only sees my huge workstation when she sleeps on the mattress in "her" room during out-of-town visits.

Downstairs, taking the covered cups and breakfast out of the refrigerator, I carefully place what my caregiver prepared for me the previous afternoon on my placemat and eat quickly. I finish packing my tote bag with my lunch, magazines, and candy or other snacks for Mom. I am typically ready well before my paratransit ride arrives. Once in a while, I am surprised when the cab or minibus shows up early or on time. Rushing out the door continues to make me nervous, even though I have met my ride hundreds of times. I usually close the back door just before the automatic lock secures my home.

I hope to arrive at the nursing home before Mom needs to go to lunch. Six days have passed, and I need to see her, talk to her, before I push her wheelchair into the dining room. I quickly tell her what I have been doing and share any tidbits of my life she may find interesting. Although I try to refrain from mentioning anything that may worry her, I am not too good at it yet. I used to tell Mom everything.

My mom's questions typically come before lunch as well. Aside from "how are you feeling?" I sometimes giggle at, but have grown to appreciate, the questions I think are frequently on her mind.

"Are you taking care of yourself?"

"Have you had any falls lately?"

"Is someone coming to help you tonight?"

"Are you eating?"

That last one reminds me of a funnier version she asked Cris two years earlier when I stayed at my sister's house during one of Mom's first hospitalizations.

"Are you feeding Stephanie?"

"What? Does she think you're starving me?" I asked Cris.

Mom did not realize our roles were beginning to reverse. None of us did. I began to feel the reversal taking place, but did not understand all it would encompass. I still have difficulties in my new role, as Mom struggles with hers. When our mother-daughter roles seemed clearer, Mom most likely had difficulties imagining a time when I could care for myself more easily than she could care for herself, or when I would worry about her as much as, or more than, she worries about me.

1
Early Childhood:
Disabilities, Possibilities

Thirty-nine years ago, I doubt my mom thought she would worry about her younger daughter living on her own one day. With one daughter, Cristina, who had turned four in early April 1973, my parents awaited the birth of their second baby toward the end of the month. When I showed no signs of wanting to come into the world, and with the doctor going on vacation, Mom headed into Bellevue Maternity Hospital in Niskayuna, New York, to be induced on April 28th.

After a short period of time, labor started, progressed quickly, and Mom delivered me. She did not hear my cry, though. Mom recalled doctors and nurses rushing in and out of the delivery room, as her physician started whacking the seven pound, blue baby on the bottom. As Miss Foley, my favorite teacher in middle school, joked with me when she asked about my birth, "You were born a Smurf!"

Baby Smurf eventually wailed.

Doctors later told my mom and dad, and Mom explained to me again and again when I became old enough to ask, that I pressed on the umbilical cord as I came down the birth canal. During those few minutes, I was deprived of oxygen, causing damage to the parts of my brain that control movement and speech. My birth would be described in my medical charts as "difficult" and "traumatic." Although I breathed on my own after the whacking, I stayed in the hospital for a few weeks as tests were administered. A spinal tap confirmed that I didn't have bleeding on the brain. Doctors casually informed my parents that I could be blind, have learning disabilities, or not have any impairments at all.

Mom always said I was a fussy infant, crying incessantly when I wouldn't, or couldn't, settle down to sleep. Nana Adele, my maternal grandmother, told me how she patiently rocked me to sleep many nights. After a few months, my parents noticed that my tiny hands were clenched in fists most of the time. My head flopped all around my shoulders. I startled at the slightest noise. Comparing my development, or lack of it, to my sister's, my mom took me, a year-old child, to the pediatrician, who referred us to a neurologist. Mom remembered that the doctor performed a cursory exam, including throwing a sheet over my head that I did not make an attempt to pull off.

He then told my mom that I had cerebral palsy.

Mom recalled that moment as one of the loneliest in her life. She had brought me to the appointment by herself. She did not know anything about cerebral palsy (CP) – never even had heard of the condition. The neurologist rattled off information about physical, occupational, and speech therapy. His recommendations included beginning these therapies immediately.

My parents received more information about my disability in the months and years ahead. CP was the brief and general diagnosis; my official diagnosis read "athetoid cerebral palsy with spastic quadriplegia." Athetoid means that I have a lot of uncontrollable, writhing movements, and quadriplegia involves these movements in both arms and legs.

While many individuals with CP are involved on one side of the body, my impairments are unusual in that my right arm and my left leg are weaker and show the most involvement. The spastic part of the diagnosis causes my muscles to tighten, and is more noticeable when I get excited or really nervous. Although I have learned to better control the spasticity, my right wrist aches from the tightness. I have to will my right fist open to grasp an object. When I really need to get a good night's sleep, a muscle relaxant helps me.

I began the triple combination of physical, occupational, and speech therapy soon after my diagnosis. Physical therapists thought I had the ability to walk, so they advised my parents not to put me in a wheelchair. One of the primary goals in my early therapy was to get me on my feet and walking. To accomplish this goal, Mom and Dad followed therapists' advice and let me stay overnight for a few weeks at a rehabilitation hospital. Pictures taken of me in the hospital, holding onto the rungs of a metal crib, show me looking like a caged animal ready to spring from confinement. And that's exactly what I did. I was not going to stay there, away from my mom and dad, for however many weeks they wanted to hold me captive. In about two weeks, I got up and started walking in my royal blue and white sneakers with toddler-sized crutches. Starting to walk had ended my captivity.

***

In addition to outpatient therapy, my parents worked with me at home. Dad encouraged me to walk outside on the grass, and when I developed better balance, I had great fun trying to strike his leg with one of my crutches! Nana Adele and Daddy George, my grandfather, helped me practice new activities.

Daddy George, who thought of the name when my toddler sister began calling him Daddy a few days after my parents went on a trip, weighted my Fisher-Price shopping cart so I wouldn't tip it over as I pushed it to walk. He and I also practiced picking up small objects when he and I would shoot marbles down an incline made of books and my Fisher-Price record player! I know I grasped the multicolored marbles with my whole hand, and not my thumb and index finger that Nana always tried to get me to use.

While on the floor, I most likely sat in the "w" position, which I was not supposed to do, even though it gave me greater stability. Still, playing with Nana and Daddy George gave me more therapy disguised as fun. Nana also took great pride in claiming to be my first speech therapist when she worked with me on learning how to say "Mom" to surprise her after my parents came home from a trip.

Ongoing PT consisted of lots of balancing exercises and learning how to catch myself before hitting the floor. My favorite involved lying on my tummy on a huge primary colored ball, rolling around as the therapist held onto me by the legs. I held out my arms and practiced pushing back with my hands while holding my head up. This exercise began to engrain the importance of holding my head up when I start to feel like I'm losing my balance. Rolling on the ball made me practice strengthening my muscles and maintaining my balance when I wasn't laughing too hard to practice the goals.

Whatever OT I had, mostly in preschool, didn't seem any fun to me. Exercises to practice manipulating small objects, buttoning oversized buttons, or trying to pull large zippers up and down became extremely frustrating. My fingers that didn't want to do any of that. Even grasping food and attempting to get it from hand to mouth didn't encourage me much. To this day, I avoid finger food as much as possible and eat almost everything with a fork. Spoons required more patience to master, but I eventually learned to feed myself cereal and chunky soups as I got older. As I received less and less OT in school, my parents worked with me improving my less than fine motor skills.

Mom's experience as an elementary school teacher led her to bring home many handwriting workbooks in which she wanted me to practice forming letters, but they mostly remained blank. My best OT exercises came much later, after high school, when I had to, or wanted to, figure out how to sign my name, apply make-up, or open my own mail.

Speech therapy was the one constant I could count on throughout school. It began as soon as I started talking because I was so difficult to understand. I kept talking, though. The one time I stopped talking happened a year or two after all of my therapy began. I pushed myself so hard to achieve goals in all of my therapies that I shut down and stopped talking.

My parents worried that I was regressing. The therapists agreed that my intense motivation to do whatever they wanted me to do was actually causing me to withdraw and stop trying. After a short break, everyone who worked with me eased me back into my routines so that I could continue making progress.

***

When I became old enough to understand that I had a disability, I saw how different I was from other children. Watching my sister play with friends made me realize what I could not do, even though I was younger than they were. Of course, as I grew up, more encounters with peers highlighted my differences.

I'm guilty of feeling sorry for myself throughout my life. I have my pity party moments. My feelings would be put into perspective many times, though, as I saw other children with CP who had more impairments than I did. Some were strapped into reclining wheelchairs, and other kids I saw during PT could only lie on a mat, moaning while a therapist tried to move their spastic arms and legs. And while I saw children with my disability who could do a lot more than I could do, or whose speech could be more easily understood, seeing kids with more severe forms of CP allowed me to begin to realize how indeed lucky I was. Reminders of how differences can affect individuals so greatly, particularly with the same diagnosis or label, helped me keep my balance between accepting my limitations and achieving my possibilities.

2

Elementary and Middle School: Learning my Differences, Joining the Mainstream

By 1978, our family moved from upstate New York to Dad's native Texas, where he continued his career as an electrical engineer at Texas Instruments in Dallas. My Kindergarten class, for orthopedically handicapped children (as we were called at the time), had seven or eight students and two teachers. To live closer to Prestonwood Elementary, where I would attend first grade, too, we soon moved across the city to Richardson. Our one-story house on Goldenrod gave me a big, back courtyard, lit with bright green lights, to ride around on my tricycle. I also had someone special I would always remember – a close friend. Dani lived two houses down the street from us. I spent afternoons with her playing school or splashing around in her brightly-colored plastic pool. She and her mom didn't care that I could not do everything she could do, or that I did some things differently.

First grade in Ms. McMichael's class introduced me to typing. Since my poor fine motor skills were incapable of producing legible handwriting, one of my educational goals became finding another way to express my thoughts on paper. When a therapist first mentioned the possibility of typing, she suggested I should use a headstick, which would allow me to type with a pointer attached to my head. My parents, particularly my mom, became adamant about not having me use this device. Mom wanted me to type with my fingers – or maybe not type at all. I could not control many of my fingers, though.

I began typing on an IBM Selectric typewriter with a metal keyguard screwed to it. The keyguard fit over the keys, giving me a surface to rest my left hand and preventing me from pressing multiple keys while aiming for one. My left thumb served as the only digit I could control precisely. To capitalize letters, I used the CAPS LOCK key. Typing special characters, however, caused much difficulty because I needed to use the SHIFT key. Using SHIFT required the ability of two fingers simultaneously; one to hold down the SHIFT key, and another to press a character. Something impossible for me to do at the time. I repeatedly worked on getting my right hand on the keyguard and using one finger to hold down SHIFT, while my left thumb hit the key I needed to strike. With my timing frequently off, my right index finger frequently released SHIFT as my left thumb tried to strike the other key! Hitting two keys at once took loads of practice. My method of typing proved too slow to keep up with my grade-level assignments. While I continued to type at school and at home, I mostly dictated my answers to teachers and to my mom and dad.

**

Our move to Houston, when Dad was transferred in 1980, brought many changes to our lives. My sister, known as Tina in her younger years, wanted a new image as Cris and started sixth grade in Catholic school. As a second grader, I attended our neighborhood school. Similar to first grade, my new class had fewer than ten students with a teacher and an aide. This class felt more separated from other students as we were taught in a temporary building beside the playground. The building, with its steep ramp access, seemed too small for us to learn subjects on many different grade levels. Being pushed up and down that ramp in my blue and white striped McLaren stroller became one of the highlights of my day.

I sat in my stroller on a mini bus that brought me to school and picked me up in the afternoon. Some days, I would go home with Dana, a pretty, plump girl in my class who used a wheelchair. Dana's grandmother greeted us at the door, gave us a snack, and let us watch the rest of *General Hospital* with her. Other times, Dana would come over to my house. Mom had trouble helping her out of her wheelchair and into our house because of the step at both the front and back doors. Once inside, we had a snack and started our homework. Although Dana and I were the same age, our math homework differed. Mine seemed more challenging.

One day, a substitute bus driver took us home. I was always the first one dropped off since I lived closer to school than Dana. I tried to tell this to the man as he drove to Dana's house. He wouldn't listen, or couldn't understand me. After Dana got dropped off, I tried to tell him where I lived and pointed in that direction. I saw the driver looking at me, with my arms flailing, in the mirror.

As he drove farther and farther in the opposite direction, I began crying. I hadn't stopped when he pulled over in front of a school and left me alone to go ask for directions. My tears almost drowned me as a group of much older boys boarded the bus, laughing and pointing at me. They got off in a hurry. I guess they figured they had the wrong bus with the screaming little crippled girl on it.

The driver finally came back to the bus with an angry look on his face. Driving back across the city took him longer than getting there. With many roads behind us, I began to recognize the houses in my neighborhood. Before the bus pulled in front of my house, I could see Mom outside. I couldn't tell which had more control over her – fear or anger. Calming me down took many hugs and much more time than my round trip across the city. The driver took me to Meadow Lake Drive all right - the continuation of the street on the opposite side of town. In the wrong zip code. Nowhere near my school.

I wished he would have tried to understand what I told him. I may have been a screaming little crippled girl, but I knew where I lived.

***

With this bus incident fresh on their minds, Mom and Dad were less than thrilled at my annual ARD (Admission, Review, and Dismissal) meeting when the school district announced plans to transfer me for fourth grade. Attending this school would involve a forty-five minute bus ride each way, and I would learn in a similar class – separated from other fourth graders. My parents wanted better for me, leading Mom to make a decision that would affect my education through high school. Having given up her teaching career after I was born, she applied to a neighboring school district. Her new position as an instructional aide allowed her to bring me into the district. I had the opportunity to attend a brand new elementary school closer to home than the one my home district wanted me to attend.

An immediate problem existed. Bringing me into the district required my parents to provide my transportation. Mom's longer workday meant that I got out of school about twenty minutes before she did. I needed to go somewhere for that twenty minutes until Mom picked me up. I remember hearing my mom on the phone calling several daycare centers, explaining my disability and my need to be picked up from school and basically sit in my stroller until she came. She made many calls until a daycare agreed to accept me.

If Cris developed a new image for herself with her name change, I developed a new image as a fourth grader. Fourth grade introduced my parents and me to a new type of educational experience – mainstreaming. For the first time, I attended a regular class. Instead of having fewer than ten classmates, I had twenty-five! I did not stay in the classroom all day, though. When Mrs. Stamm began teaching math, for example, I went to the resource room. Mrs. Blizzard helped me with the same math problems my classmates were doing. As she wrote my work, I learned to do lots of calculations in my head. Whenever I couldn't type assignments in class, I went to resource for assistance. This room became very familiar to me for many reasons.

A one-story building, Heflin Elementary had carpet almost everywhere. Although my dad pushed me to class in my stroller in the morning (because he was late much of the time), I used my walker in the building. I walked independently when I stopped using crutches. But everyone agreed that I needed to use a walker in school. I pushed my walker to the resource room, to speech therapy, and to the cafeteria, which excited me because I ate lunch with all of the fourth graders. My walker and I went to the gym, where

I participated in PE - to an extent - with my class, square dancing during Rodeo and hanging onto parallel bars with help from one of the teachers. I didn't like leaving my friends to go and do exercises by myself whenever I happened to have adaptive PE. Although PT also pulled me away from my classmates, I didn't mind having therapy in these neat little caves where the therapist would work with me on an exercise mat. As a class, we went into these caves and read together. Of course, my walker went with me as well.

My class took a trip down the hall one day to visit a class called SMH. Going to visit this class, which I later learned stood for Severely Multiply Handicapped, provided an opportunity to see students quite different from us. Mrs. Stamm reminded us to be on our best behavior as she led our line.

"Do not make fun of anyone. Talk to these students the way you talk to your friends."

We entered the large room with blue mats on the floor. Some kids were lying down; others were strapped into cushioned wheelchairs. One or two children kept crying, which sounded more like moaning. I looked closely at a little girl on one of the mats. I thought she looked like me, with short hair and a small body frame. Her name was Dolly. She was around my age.

"Hi, Dolly. I like your name. I have a little white dog named Dolly."

I didn't know what else to say. I think I touched her hand, which was cold. She startled, and one of her bent legs jerked a little. Mine did that, too, at times. I saw that she wore a diaper. The smell of it bothered me. In fact, the entire room made me feel queasy with the smell of dirty diapers. My friends and I walked around the room a few more minutes. As my class left, I looked back at Dolly, who stared at the ceiling.

Each time my class passed the SMH room, I thought about Dolly on the mat.

***

After school, the KinderCare bus picked me up with other students and took a short drive to the day care center. On half days, or when my mom had to stay late at school, I got out of my stroller and played. On typical days, though, I remained in my stroller and drank juice through a straw. Sometimes, I looked at a book one of the workers gave me. Once, through earphones that were too large and clumsy to stay on my wobbly head, I followed along with a book on tape. I overheard one of the workers remark, "She's actually following along with the words in the book!"

"Well, I am in fourth grade. I do know how to read," I wanted to reply. I didn't think they would understand me, however, and I just wanted to see Mom walk through the door and go home.

My daily twenty or so minutes in after-school daycare only lasted a year. My mom's instructional aide position was cut at her school. She transferred in the same position to another school – Heflin! She ended up taking Mrs. Blizzard's job when my resource teacher became a classroom teacher. In fifth grade, I went to school with Mom and saw her when I went to the resource room for extra help. After school, I hung out in her room until she took us home. While I liked knowing Mom was in the same building, seeing her in the hallway gave me the feeling that she was always watching me!

***

Every few years, I was pulled out of class to be tested. These tests allowed me to keep receiving special education services while participating in the regular classroom. In fact, having been tested in various settings since preschool, I grew accustomed to these sessions. That year, I began being tested by Mrs. Grothaus, my speech pathologist. She worked with me on the part in which I would repeat words, describe pictures, and tell her which choice of answers came next in a sequence. When we finished in her small room, Mrs. Grothaus called the diagnostician and walked with me to her office.

In the diagnostician's office, she and I worked on academic types of tests. I read to her, finished sentences, spelled both real and nonsense words, and answered math questions. One test involved reading one word per page. With each turn of a page, words became more indecipherable. After a while, I didn't recognize many words, and I certainly couldn't pronounce them. I became worried and frustrated.

"How about this word?"

I stared at it. "I don't know."

"How about this one?"

Again, I tried to figure it out. "I don't know," I almost cried.

After several minutes, the diagnostician stopped turning pages. She looked at me and said, "Stephanie, you're not supposed to know these words. I had to get a certain number of 'I don't knows' before we could stop. This is the farthest I have gotten in this book with any student."

With that reassurance, and mostly straight 'A's' on my report cards, I began middle school.

***

As a sixth grader at Killough Middle School, I had a later morning schedule than my mom. With Dad traveling internationally in his job, Mom needed help driving me back and forth to school. Living by herself in Florida, Nana Adele offered to move in with us and help. Sharing a room, Nana and I became close, very quickly.

While my friends who lived in the school district were assigned to middle schools, administrators and my parents discussed which school would work best for me. Since we lived out of district, I needed my own transportation no matter which school I attended. Killough had only one floor, and again, lots of carpet. My stroller still transported me into the building, and remained in my homeroom until the afternoon rush. Many of my friends from Heflin went to Killough, including Trisha from Mrs. Stamm's class. Mrs. Stamm went, too! She taught me math again.

A few days before school started, Nana and I went to meet my teachers and learn the location of my classes. Sixth graders were grouped in pods. In Pod "C," my classmates and I remained together most of the day. During seven class periods, we had math with Mrs. Stamm, language arts with Mrs. Theis (or 'The Is' to remember how to spell her name), and science with Miss Foley. While Nana and I met most of my teachers on a brief tour of the school, I had a preview of becoming the most teased sixth grader by Miss Foley.

"You're not going to hit me with that walker, are you?"

"No. Not yet."

Becoming accustomed to Foley's sense of humor took a while before I knew how to take it and give it right back. I soon answered to her name for me, "Tornado" or "Tornado Child," and called my teacher by her last name only. We developed a friendship beyond that of teacher and student. When I acted obnoxious, however, she called me on it. She also supported me through the typical, and not so typical, first year of middle school challenges, taping a bouquet of flowers on my walker one morning after a particularly rough day.

Seven periods meant a faster pace in class and in the hallways. As an elective, good students could become BOAs (Business Office Assistants) during one period a day, helping in the office or library, or assisting individual teachers. Or, in my case, helping me with written class assignments. One of my favorite BOA's, an eighth grader named Leigh, helped me in Mrs. Theis' class. She then left class with me a few minutes early. We walked to the slippery tiled cafeteria, where Leigh brought me a regular chair to sit in at the end of the bench-lined tables and opened my lunch.

I continued to go to the resource room for extra assistance with longer assignments and tests. While I took as many regular electives as I could, including theatre arts, speech, and art, one period was always reserved for adaptive PE. With three to four students in my class, we did more than mat exercises. Our teacher and her aide led us in ball games and allowed us to play on the elementary school playground next door. We took walks outside, and learned how to avoid bumps and curbs, particularly when Lisa, who had CP, too, drove her motorized wheelchair off a curb. Individually, the teacher and I worked on walking up and down the carpeted library ramp, and climbing stairs.

Middle school included a weekly hour of speech therapy, or Communication Skills. When the district provided them for me, I attended additional sessions of speech and PT in summer school. During summer school, speech went beyond the reading of boring passages to make clearer 'm' and 's' sounds. Once, my therapist made therapy fun by allowing me to call my friend Trisha and practice speaking clearly and breathing between every few words. Learning how to breathe more air into my lungs, however, didn't seem fun or as relaxing as it was supposed to be. Although I lay down on a mat while listening to instructions on breathing deeply, a therapist whom I didn't know well kept pushing me to move my diaphragm up and down. I couldn't get it to rise and fall in conjunction with my breaths. Instead of becoming more and more relaxed, I became increasingly frustrated. Her hand pressing on my abdomen didn't help. Finally, I couldn't try anymore and started crying. She told me I could stop and went to get my mom, waiting outside the small room. Mom didn't understand what happened. On the way home, I explained how uncomfortable and frustrated I became, mostly with myself. At the next session, the therapist worked with me on the mat again. This time, however, she took it easier on me and asked me to tell her if I became frustrated.

Each school year, I received less and less PT. I rarely saw an OT. My mom and dad wanted me to have as much PT as possible, so Lou became my Wednesday afternoon companion. After school, I came home and received a weekly hour of private PT. Lou started out on the living room carpet having me lift my legs with weights strapped to my ankles. I then got on my hands and knees to lift and straighten one leg at a time. Repetitions followed with my arms, too. My hour always ended with walking around the atrium in our house. I couldn't get away with my usual walking, though.

"Head up, heels down. Swing your arms naturally. Slow down," Lou would instruct me.

Nana watched me walk on the unpolished Mexican tile around the atrium. "See, you can do it. I want to see that good walking all the time." This 'perfect' walking slowed me down! I would hear many more reminders from Mom, Dad, and Nana.

"What did Lou teach you?"

"Walk like a soldier."

"Stephanie, put your arms down and your head up. Your feet will move without you looking at them!"

My favorite came from Mom. "We paid all of that money for therapy. I want to see how Lou taught you to walk." Those words would guilt me into slowing down and walking better – for a while!

***

Seventh grade brought similar academic arrangements with BOA's in class, shortened assignments, and time in the resource room. That year, I became a BOA. One semester, I helped Foley, Mrs. Stamm, and other sixth grade teachers in their classrooms. I learned how to clean an overhead without drenching myself and did whatever else teachers thought I could do to help. Being a BOA, rather than just receiving help from one, made me feel useful. Of course, I think Foley arranged this period to force me to put up with more of her teasing, and I enjoyed every minute of it!

An elective I took introduced me to this radical machine called the personal computer. I still typed periodically on my typewriter, and my skills – or lack of them – transferred to the PC. Just as my typing would have been nonexistent without a typewriter keyguard, my typing on a computer required a keyguard. My first PC keyguard, a UPS-brown, heavy plastic board, attached to the keyboard with Velcro. To stabilize the keyboard, therapists put Dycem, a rubber-like material, under it. Typing continued to be painfully slow. I took every computer class offered and became computer literate while trying to improve my physical skills.

With more hands-on learning in seventh grade science, Mr. Wall's class seemed challenging. Since everyone had lab partners, though, I didn't feel singled out when I couldn't manipulate lab trays. I worked harder to concentrate on what my classmates did with the equipment and samples. My concentration paid off unexpectedly.

My parents came to my annual ARD meeting to review my progress and discuss my goals for the next school year. I usually didn't see them when they came; I was always in class. This year, however, they walked through the halls. That day, I noticed Mom talking to my Texas History teacher, who showed my mom her grade book.

Okay, so I messed up on the last test. I still maintained a 'B' average!

That night, Mom told me I was receiving a seventh grade award.

"But I'm not doing that great in history."

"You're doing fine. She showed me the other students' grades. You put too much pressure on yourself."

On Award's Night, I was confused. Why would my history teacher be awarding a 'B' average?

Mr. Wall rose and spoke about a student who worked so hard in class. "This student starts to get upset when she doesn't understand something. I see her get more focused until she knows it. The seventh grade science award for my class goes to Stephanie Torreno."

How embarrassing! I thought I was receiving an award in Texas History.

That surprise in seventh grade made up for the fact that I got run into by another student in the hallway. Although this incident wasn't my first knockdown, I have reason to remember it. Someone helped me stand up, then walked with me to the counselor's office. I felt the knot on my temple, and a few minutes later, I threw up everywhere. The feeling of embarrassment that often accompanied me elevated off the charts that day.

***

Just as Mrs. Stamm became a two-time teacher of mine, my last year of middle school gave me another two-time teacher. I'm not sure whether Foley arranged to teach eighth grade science, or if I got lucky, or on a few days, unlucky. Foley and I had a teacher-student friendship one last time. She not only played jokes on me, but also used me to trick others.

If not having total control over my arms and legs wasn't enough to manage, I contended with loose shoulders. Both shoulders "came out." My parents and I learned from an orthopedic surgeon that the tendons in my shoulders caused partial dislocations. Whether or not these uncomfortable episodes were caused by my abnormal movements, they made my arms more uncontrollable. I couldn't do much with an arm just hanging out. Surgery could correct this problem, but the doctor didn't recommend it because my CP would prevent me from remaining still enough to heal during recovery. So, I began to say "my arm is out" frequently at home and at school. Most of the time, I worked my arm "in" again, but if I couldn't, my teachers applied gentle pressure to my shoulder or called the school nurse.

Once, Foley came to me before class and said, "In the middle of class, I want you to act like your shoulder has come out. We are going to play a trick on David."

I hardly controlled my giggling. I didn't know why Foley wanted to make David her target that day or what she had up her sleeve, but I kept my eyes locked on hers throughout science. Finally, when she paused in the middle of teaching, I raised my hand.

"Miss Foley, my arm is out. I can't get it back in," I tried to sound scared to make it believable.

Foley rushed over to my table. She rubbed my shoulder a little; I couldn't even look at her.

"David, use the wall phone. Tell the office we need the nurse here."

David stood his tall body up and walked over to grab the phone. Picking up the receiver, his ear became covered with petroleum jelly! I couldn't keep it in any longer and burst out laughing. Foley hollered her favorite word, "Psych!"

For all of the fun we had that year, it also became one of the toughest.

***

On a January afternoon, an announcement came over the PA system. "Will all students who were in sixth grade, pod "C" two years ago meet in the cafeteria right away?" I think I was in an elective at the other end of the building, away from eighth grade academics. Walking to the center of the school took me longer than other students. As I approached the tile floor of the cafeteria, I heard the principal speaking. I slowed down to avoid making too much noise with my walker. I saw Foley quickly get up to meet me halfway. She wasn't smiling.

"I forgot about you, Stephanie. I wanted to tell you privately. Miss Theis died last night."

My legs began to shake underneath me. She helped me reach a table and chair against the windows in the middle of the hallway. I sat down and started crying. Foley and I kept sitting together as my friends were dismissed and started walking back to class. Most were crying, too.

Miss Theis, who became Mrs. McCaleb when she remarried the year before, lost her battle with cancer. She had two children around my age.

Foley walked me to Nana's car that afternoon. I tried to concentrate on my homework when I got home. Mom and I talked a lot that night. I felt better going to school the next morning. When the morning announcements came on, however, and mentioned Mrs. McCaleb, I cried all over again in math. Foley came in the classroom, plopped me in her teacher's chair with wheels, and took me to a conference room. I knew I had to get control over myself, but I thought of someone else, too.

I told Foley that Mom began undergoing treatment for precancerous uterine cells. After some abnormal Pap tests, Mom's school nurse told her she needed to see a gynecologist, not just a general practitioner. This advice saved her life. As an emotional eighth grader, though, losing a teacher so young to cancer made me worry about Mom.

In addition to my worries about Mom, my fears about starting high school began to grip me. Foley talked to me about how different school life would be as a "little fish in the big blue sea." She kept trying to prepare me. I needed to toughen up, she would say, and I knew she was right. Her message in my yearbook gave me a sense of the confidence she had in me, even if I didn't have it in myself.

"Well – we made it! Through three years together and I know this was the toughest. I just hope high school is great for you and I know you're ready for it," Foley wrote.

In May, my parents attended my final middle school ARD meeting. At home, Mom and Dad always shared comments from teachers and therapists. When my teachers complimented me on my study habits and work ethic, Mom told me how Dad informed teachers of the one afternoon break I took before I tackled my homework. He explained my ritual of watching the taped recording of *All My Children* with Cris after school. We even fast-forwarded commercials to cut show time down to forty-five minutes. Unlike my sister, I didn't try to start homework until the show ended, though!

I really appreciated Dad telling this secret during the meeting. Foley enjoyed teasing me about watching a soap opera.

***

With all of the emotions I experienced that year, eighth grade ended on two high notes. Dad took me to the eighth grade dance, the only school dance I ever attended. My nerves about dancing in my black patent leather dress shoes on the slick cafeteria tile didn't stop me from joining the fun. I danced with groups of friends, some of whom I knew since our days at Heflin together.

On Award's Night, Mom, Dad, Nana, and Cris watched as I received the Presidential Academic Fitness

Award. Foley made my night when she handed me the certificate and said, "President Reagan told me to give this to you."

Foley and I continued to hang out for many years. I reminded myself of her advice while swimming in the big sea of high school. Before going to that sea, though, I had fun in some real water.

3
Summers with Nana: Taking the Bus, Going to Paradise

My three months of summer vacation became more fun when Nana Adele came to live with us. When I began middle school, I stopped going to summer school for PT and speech. Enough was enough! Dad always wanted me to go to overnight camp, but I was afraid to go where I didn't know anyone. I didn't like the idea of strangers taking care of me. One summer, I did go to a day camp for children with disabilities. I remember talking to the counselors more than the other campers.

As Nana began packing to return to her home in Florida at the end of her first school year in Houston, Mom suggested that I go with her. I, of course, thought spending the summer with her was a great idea. What better way to spend the summer? Hanging out at the beach, swimming in a salt-water pool, walking through the sand. Now we started talking about my kind of physical therapy!

***

Nana Adele and Daddy George bought their one bedroom condominium in Palm Beach, Florida after my mom graduated from college in the mid-1960s. The Palm Beach White House, the name of their condominium building, became their winter home to escape the New York snow. Nana's parents usually joined them, sleeping on the hideaway bed in the living room. My mom often vacationed at the condo, on the first floor of the three-story building, which stood perpendicular to the beach. In fact, Mom told me she first felt me fluttering like a butterfly in her tummy on a late summer morning in August 1972 while visiting Nana.

After they sold their Long Island home on a golf course, Nana and Daddy George considered the condo their permanent home. With Daddy George's death on Christmas Day in 1980, and my great-grandmother's death a few years later, Nana lived alone. As she began spending the school year with us, Nana decided to rent the condo during the winter.

Only one "problem" existed in our perfect summer plans. Nana was terrified of flying.

I flew many times on family vacations. Travelling in the air to quickly reach a destination didn't scare me. Nana, on the other hand, did not even want to entertain the idea of flying a few hours to Palm Beach.

"Nana, I'll hold your hand. Maybe you can take something to calm you down, too."

"No, I can't do it. I will die of fright in the air."

29

Nothing I did or said convinced my grandmother to fly. No, she and I took her preferred mode of long-distance transportation. We went Greyhound, and left the driving to them!

The trip from the Houston bus station to the West Palm Beach terminal took over thirty hours. Although the time on the road shortened a little each year, every minute seemed excruciating to me. I loved being with Nana, but I hated sitting in a cramped space for hours at a time. My body despised it even more. Every muscle stiffened. Nana let me rest my head on her lap to help me fall asleep at night. It really didn't help me relax, though, as I always felt as though I was slipping to the floor. Whenever I did fall asleep, the bus stopped at a station, and the driver turned on the bright lights.

"Everybody off the bus. It has to be cleaned."

Nana and I tried to get the driver to let us stay on the bus each time this happened during the night. We never had any luck. Walking my stiff body into a bus station without falling required waking my sleepy self – quickly. Just entering a bus terminal in the black of night gave me the creeps. I simply wanted to go to the restroom where Nana didn't allow me to touch anything - with good reason - and board the bus again.

Morning finally arrived. Since we ate all of the food Nana brought with us, we had an early breakfast at one of the first stops in the Sunshine State. Nana had trouble walking in her high heels because her feet swelled. She explained to me that if she took her shoes off during the night, she would never get them back on in the morning. Never mind that she shouldn't have been wearing three-inch heels on a bus in the first place!

Nana always let me sit in the seat next to the window. The first sights of palm trees and orange groves heightened my anticipation for the next eight weeks. Looking out the window and talking to other passengers made the time pass, but not quickly enough for me. I wanted to reach our destination and begin summer in paradise.

Our road trip finally came to an end when the Greyhound bus pulled into the West Palm Beach station in the late afternoon of a long day. Nana's longtime neighbors and good friends, Edna and Ralph, always picked us up. We then went out for a quick dinner at the same buffet-style restaurant each year, The Holiday House. Nana and Edna did most of the talking, something I became used to in the coming weeks. Ralph asked me a few questions. Since neither Edna nor Ralph understood my speech very well, we mostly just smiled at one another. I didn't have much energy to talk anyway.

The moment I had been waiting for came when we were on the way to the condo. Ralph drove his long white Cadillac across the intracoastal bridge from West Palm to the island of Palm Beach. The street lights in the dark sky allowed me to still see the tall palms on either side of South Ocean Boulevard. As Ralph pulled into the first driveway, the familiar layout of the two white buildings facing each other, around parking spaces and a median of grass, told me I was home for the summer. Getting out of the car, I immediately smelled the ocean air and heard the ocean waves rolling onto shore. If we didn't feel exhausted, I would have dragged Nana on the short walk to the swimming pool deck overlooking the Atlantic Ocean. On Nana's side of the condominium complex, I saw the private balconies. Nana's balcony became a haven whenever I wanted a great view of the ocean.

Recovering from our two-day journey and settling into a comfortable routine took a few days. Nana didn't keep a car there, so we relied on Edna and Ralph and other neighbors to take us to the grocery store, to church, or wherever else we needed to go. One of Nana's friends, Ilene, took us grocery shopping at Publix or Winn Dixie.

Ilene frequently shared memories of her daughter with me. Her daughter, who had mild CP, had gotten married and had children. She died of cancer many years before I met Ilene. Hearing about her daughter's life first awakened me to the realization that people with CP married and had children.

Most of our days in Palm Beach revolved around going to the pool. I impatiently waited while Nana finished her daily routines before we headed to the water.

"Nana, why can't we eat lunch while we watch *All My Children?*"

"I'm always up and down getting something from the kitchen. I miss too much."

"You have a dishwasher, Nana. Why can't we use it?"

"We only have a few dishes. I'll wash them by hand. It will only take a few minutes."

By the time Nana's few minutes passed, and she sat down to look at the newspaper, the clock hit 2:30. Putting on our bathing suits took more time, as did walking and climbing six wide steps to the pool deck. The best few hours of my summer day finally began.

Once we settled down at the poolside table under the avocado green umbrella, I couldn't wait to use the handrail to walk down the steps into the pool. I reluctantly wore floaties that allowed me to jump, kick, and swim however I wanted. Most days, we enjoyed the pool to ourselves or shared it with just a few other year-round residents. Other summers, we met people visiting from Europe or from other parts of the world. As I became older and more self-conscious, I abandoned my floaties and sat on the steps or held onto the railing around the pool to kick and exercise my legs. I received plenty of PT – without any therapists!

Although I always wanted to stay in the pool for hours, I enjoyed getting out and standing under the open air shower that separated the pool deck from the sand of the beach. The blazing hot sun dried me off. We watched sailboats and motor boats, along with the occasional cruise ship in the distance, drift along the blue-green waters. If Nana had let me, I would have sat on the deck until dark, watching the rippling waves rolling to shore.

Nana and I walked to the ocean once in a while. She seemed a little afraid of going to the shore with me alone. I understood her apprehension. Walking on the white powdery sand challenged my balance and stamina. I walked better when I kept my shoes on which I had to do to prevent my feet from burning. Once I reached the shore, though, I had difficulty taking off my shoes without sitting down or leaning on something. When I managed to take my shoes off, I loved walking on the smooth wet sand and feeling the water roll between my toes. It was a real treat to keep my balance and not land on the burning sand while I walked on the sloping beach! Occasionally, people we met at the pool or friends we saw each summer, including the Simons and their granddaughter, Andrea, went with us and provided more assistance.

Rainy days tested me. Sometimes, I convinced Nana that the sky didn't really look that dark and that the clouds were passing. We got caught in the rain a few times because neither one of us attempted to run. Our bathing suits served their purpose. On other days, I had to be content watching the rain come down between the swaying palms. I made sure I saved the books I brought to keep me occupied those days. When I ran out of my books, I always counted on Edna and Ralph to share the Palm Beach Post and the tabloids with me. Mom sent many care packages with magazines from home, too.

When Nana went next door to visit Edna, I treasured the time to myself - a lot of time. The two friends talked and talked and lost track of time. I frequently wondered what they chatted about for hours. Alone, I turned up my pop music on the pink cassette player and radio. I often went out on the balcony and stretched out on the lounge chairs. Through the lattice design of the dark red bricks under the white concrete railing, I watched cars and people come and go in the parking lot. Standing against the railing, I had an expansive view of the ocean to the left. To the right, the building that stood across the boulevard faced the intracoastal waterway. From the same vantage point, Nana and I watched the fireworks on Independence Day.

During a few summers, Mom visited us for a week. I loved seeing her because I missed her so much. Her visit also broke up our routine. Mom and I went to the pool or to the beach in the morning, then we returned in the afternoon. When she came, Mom rented a car and took us to the mall or to the exclusive shops on Worth Avenue. On Sunday, we attended mass at St. Edward's, and went to brunch at the Breakers Hotel. Afterward, Mom drove us up and down South Ocean to look at the mansions. I often remembered the names of different mansions from the plaques that hung from the brick or stucco entrances. When I wondered aloud how the winter residents crossed the busy boulevard to go to the ocean, Nana told me that many had built underground tunnels for that very reason.

My summer with Nana would not be complete without a trip to the Palm Beach Kennel Club. The gamblers in Nana, Edna, and Ralph showed me a good time when we went for dinner at the dog races. Being underage, I wasn't allowed to go to the windows to place any bets. Nana taught her "strategies" for picking numbers and placed bets for me, mostly spending all of her money in the first race! I don't think we ever left with more money than we had when we came, but we had a good time. As for my parents, I'm not sure how they felt about Nana influencing me in her corrupt ways!

The two months in Palm Beach went by faster than a few weeks in school. Soon, Nana began touching up the balcony furniture with white paint and tidying the condominium for the renters. I knew what came next – another long bus ride home. This time, I anticipated seeing Mom and Dad. I had tanned skin, blonder hair, and great memories to share with them.

4
High School:
Growing through the Lows,
Holding my Head up High

Whatever independence and confidence I gained in middle school withstood testing throughout high school. My adopted district had two high schools. Both were large two-story campuses each having over a thousand students. Before I graduated from Killough, I knew I would attend Hastings High in the fall of 1987.

Incoming freshmen toured the school before the first day of class. Dad brought me and walked with me as I struggled to keep up with the group. If any doubt existed about whether I could walk to my classes, this preview of campus confirmed I could not. Hastings was divided into two houses: North and South. Although my academic classes were located in North House, some of my electives took place in Hastings South, or somewhere between the two. For safety concerns and to keep me on time for classes, I used a wheelchair pushed by a paraprofessional aide, who assisted me in class, too. Before school began, my parents and I met my teachers and discussed modifications. All of this, along with meeting special education staff, already made me feel like I was treading deep water.

On the first day of school, Mom put a little make-up on me, brushed my hair, and reminded me to "sit up straight in the wheelchair. Keep your head up."

I needed to heed that advice to prevent myself from drowning over the next four years.

My aide brought the wheelchair out to my dad's car each day. With my book bag and lunch balanced on the handles, she whisked me off to first period. With my chronically late dad driving me to school within minutes of the first bell, I felt sorry for my aide having to rush to navigate me through the crowded halls. More often than not, first period involved an elevator ride and a long walk to class.

Since the faculty did not want me to tape lectures, and because I'm a visual learner, classmates used NCR paper to share notes with me. A "set" of paper included three copies; white, yellow, and pink. My note taker and I each received a copy, while some teachers saved the other copy for an absent student. One of my note takers told me she saw her biology notes being read by another student in gym! I always enjoyed knowing when my accommodations helped others as well.

Peer note takers relieved an aide from having to sit in class with me. When I needed to write independent work, however, the aide stayed with me. I soon overcame the awkwardness and embarrassment as the only student with an adult sitting beside me in class. I had many other difficulties with this arrangement.

Although my aides were required to have at least a high school diploma, many didn't seem to have basic knowledge in the subjects I took. While understanding the coursework wasn't their job, aides had great difficulties spelling both common words and unfamiliar vocabulary. Their difficulties caused me frustration in that I often had to spell many words while dictating my answers. I frequently allowed my frustration to get the best of me. Their work, however, reflected my learning and knowledge, and I wanted my work to demonstrate my intelligence. Although I received additional time on tests, having to spell every few words required much time and enormous physical effort.

Working with aides in math classes included the most challenges. With classwork and tests in Algebra I and Algebra II, for instance, I needed to explain how to write every step of an equation. As a student, I realized knowing exactly how to "write" an equation was my responsibility, but having to tell someone to write each little symbol added to the complicated process.

"Open parenthesis, x squared minus...."

"X squared?"

"Yes, x with a little '2' in the air."

I tried to point to my notes or my book to communicate what I wanted written on classwork. As the subject became more difficult, dictating my answers became more physically challenging. At home, with Dad's help, we solved equations easily and quickly. He understood what I dictated, and he knew I understood the work. Doing my algebra homework with my dad at the end of a long, tiring day eased the frustrations I felt in school.

My first semester of sophomore year offered a different experience. Mrs. Knotabart, my aide, and I clicked! She knew how to write geometry, as well as my other subjects. When I lost points on a history test because I wasn't in the room to see the essay question on the board, she mentioned it to my teacher and I received the points on my grade. The essay question was written on the next test. I looked forward to going to school that semester and working with Mrs. Knotabart. After she left the position at the end of the semester to care for her children, my frustration and anxiety once again accompanied me to school.

Even between classes, my nerves took over as I needed help in the restroom. Although I needed minimal help at home, if any, I needed assistance with buttons and zippers if I wasn't wearing pull-on pants. Locking the stall door at school was difficult, so an OT made a button with a magnet that read "In use." I never used it, though, because I didn't think girls rushing in and out of stalls would see it or bother to read it. So, my aide held the swinging door closed. Requiring this type of help, and only having a few minutes for this break, didn't make using the restroom simple. Bringing a thermos of water to drink throughout the morning forced me to go with the flow!

Mom continued to give me pep talks in the morning. When tears welled up in my eyes as she did my make-up, she reminded me of what I already knew.

"School is your job, just as teaching is mine. You have to be strong and get through the day as best you can."

***

In my junior year, my biology teacher called her students' parents during the semester. When our phone rang on a Saturday evening, I never expected Dad would talk to Mrs. Fleming. Overhearing part of their conversation, I listened as my father discussed my study habits and grades with the teacher. I knew I was doing well in her class, but I wondered what specifically she shared with Dad.

"Yes, that was the project about the humpback whale. We helped her write the notecards as she researched it. She told us she had to share what she learned with the class. We knew Stephanie would feel nervous speaking in front of the class, so her mom and I encouraged her to practice with us."

Dad smiled at me as he listened to my teacher. Then, he began to explain my primary difficulties in her class.

"Mrs. Fleming, Stephanie struggles as she dictates her answers on quizzes and tests. Her aide doesn't know how to spell the vocabulary. Spelling each word becomes tedious and frustrates her. She knows the material. Working with her aide to put it on paper is the problem."

My teacher agreed with Dad and told him not to have me spell words when giving my answers. Mrs. Fleming said she would figure out what the aide wrote.

Good luck with that, I thought, after my dad shared what she said.

Dad told me Mrs. Fleming said I was the only student who memorized her speech.

"I didn't want to drop my notecards in front of the class."

***

Dad frequently visited school to advocate for more modifications on classwork and homework. My homework, particularly algebra, was reduced to every other problem. As frustrated as I felt at school, my mom and dad (and Nana) were equally as frustrated with writing hours of homework each afternoon and night. No doubt, they wanted to help me and give me access to as equal an education as other students. Why did everything need to be written, though? Why couldn't I read the material without having to "copy" answers out of a textbook? My parents and I knew that if I read it as thoroughly as I had taught myself to do, I would remember the important information.

Watching my daily recording of *All My Children* continued to serve as my daily after-school break. Reading, studying, and finishing hours of work occupied the remainder of my afternoon and evening. Completing written homework, though, became a family affair.

My parents' ongoing advocacy culminated at the end of each school year at my ARD meeting. Sitting in class, I wondered what was going on among school personnel and my mom and dad. At the end of freshman or sophomore year, my parents told me that discussions became heated. The head of Special Ed remarked, "Well, if you don't like what we're doing with Stephanie, you need to take her to school in your own district."

Mom and Dad toured the school I would attend in the district where we lived. They did not like what they saw. For better or worse, I remained at Hastings.

***

Electives provided some independence. As a freshman, I took art. Since Mr. Williams recently taught another student with severe CP, accommodating my needs did not challenge him. He taped paper to the table and allowed me to create whatever I could. If an assignment seemed too complicated, such as drawing a picture using the stippling technique, he created an alternative. Rather than creating a drawing with differently spaced dots, I filled in an outline of a picture he drew. Some of my dots appeared obviously larger than others!

As a sophomore required to take a health course, I rolled into class on the first day. Before class began, my aide asked the teacher if students were going to do any writing beside note taking during class. "They're going to fill out some basic information for me," she asked. "Why?"

"I need help," I piped in, "because I can't write."

41

"You can't write?" I suspected she wanted to ask why I couldn't, but I don't think she was that clueless. I wasn't positive, though!

That first day ended as my last day in her class. My new health teacher, a coach, knew a little about me from his wife, who taught at Heflin. She had gotten to know my mom and had undoubtedly heard about my struggles.

"Don't give Stephanie written homework. Assign reading, but no written homework!"

Coach didn't even want me to highlight important information, instead of summarizing it, in a health article we brought each week. "Just read it. I'll ask you about it."

I always prepared myself for questions. Most of the time, he collected it from me and we discussed the article as a class. I made sure he knew I had read it.

Other electives gave me an outlet for my physical frustrations with academics. Special Ed typing let me practice my keyboarding skills without the pressures and impossibilities of keeping up in a regular class. As my classmates learned how to type the typical way, I continued to type with my left thumb. The teacher correctly assumed that my method was the one that worked for me, so she gave me individualized assignments and graded based on accuracy, not speed. I took other special education electives, such as Career Exploration, as well. The curriculum did not challenge me, but I enjoyed these classes as a balance to a rigorous academic load.

From my freshman year until I worshipped my senior status, ADPE came during fourth period. ADPE offered my only exercise most of the time during the school year, since I had little time for private PT anymore. The same physical therapist I had at Heflin, as well as an occupational therapist, visited me in class for a monthly consult. I did not receive much therapy. The therapy I did receive came from the ADPE teacher, who continued to work with me on walking up and down stairs, in between riding a stationary bike and doing floor exercises.

My continuing biweekly speech therapy sessions pulled me out of ADPE, since I couldn't, and didn't want to, miss any other class. I often felt I would have been more productive if I stayed in ADPE. Mrs. Roberts usually spent half of my thirty minute sessions on the phone. During the brief amount of time she worked with me, I read a passage about Native American Sacagawea until I almost recalled it verbatim. Each Tuesday and Thursday, I reported to Dad how much therapy I actually received. Sitting in the room, wasting time and not receiving much therapy, meant my dad visited school regularly. Mrs. Roberts, the only speech pathologist at Hastings at the time, and I grew to have a very uncomfortable relationship. In my junior year, I received a little more varied, and consistent, instruction with another speech pathologist.

Since ADPE always met before lunch, my classmates and I ate together. Aside from the three or four of us having various disabilities, we did not share much else in common. We sat at a table off to the side of the cafeteria with a few other tables around us. Although I would have felt uncomfortable sitting in the middle of the crowded, loud room, I wanted to join friends from other classes. I often watched an ADPE classmate, who was blind, eat and joke with his sighted buddy. They looked like they had fun. At my table, I tried to eat slowly and hoped time passed quickly.

***

Senior year finally arrived. Although I already felt apprehensive about life after high school and my desire to go to college, I looked forward to making it through the year. If my semester with Mrs. Knotabart as my aide was the best, my last two semesters rated second best. I had a good aide, supportive teachers, and a slightly more relaxed schedule. Some of the modifications that my parents fought so hard for finally helped me work more independently.

I had a choice in which math class to take, so I took computer math. That choice relieved the frustration in dictating work. I did not know if I could keep up by typing in class myself, but I did – the teacher maintained a relaxed class schedule. During my second year of taking Spanish, the teacher understood the difficulties in dictating answers to my aide, who didn't know the language. So, on quizzes and tests, she allowed me to tape record my answers in an adjacent empty classroom. I recorded homework, too, and she even gave me extra credit for singing a song, not just reciting lyrics!

Mr. Lowery taught my favorite class, English. I don't remember why I was not in his class until the second or third day of school. Maybe I scared another teacher! When I joined his class, however, I knew it would become my favorite. On one of the walls, Mr. Lowery had painted a huge sign which read, "Life is Unfair." Whenever one of my classmates would complain about homework, he said nothing. He simply pointed to the sign. The sign moved with us to the computer lab when we typed our research papers. Again, I typed my own work most of the time, and my aide took over when I became tired or needed speed. At the end of the year, Mr. Lowery painted all of his students' last names to create a border around those words. He talked to me about the rest of that message when I saw him a few times after high school.

The one glitch of senior year came when I needed to take the SAT. I would not be able to take the test on a Saturday as other seniors did, since I needed writing assistance and extended time. Instead, I missed ADPE each day for a week to take the exam. The new head of the special education department wrote for me. By the middle of the day, I already felt tired. As in my classes, the math section included most of my difficulties with dictating answers. Although I became pretty accurate in performing calculations in my head, the steps to algebraic equations and geometry problems required detailed writing. While I prepared by practicing with sample tests at home, I lacked confidence taking the exam. A few months later, I received an average score in the mail. I decided not to retake it.

I ended up not worrying too much about my SAT score. A postcard delivered to me during school one day reported that I would graduate in the top ten percent of my high school class. All of my frustrations, hard work, and determination to prove myself in class after class paid off!

One final ARD took place toward the end of school. This time, I enjoyed missing class to attend the meeting with my parents. A few members of the special education department participated, including my physical therapist and a speech pathologist from another school. Everyone shared some recommendations for my future and my plans to go to college.

My physical therapist recommended keeping up my exercise routine with walking and riding my adult-sized tricycle. She warned against gaining weight as that would make everything I tried to do more difficult. The recommendation makes me giggle now. I have not weighed as much as the 100 pounds I weighed in high school since I was nineteen.

Someone mentioned looking at small colleges, including Houston Baptist University, a small campus that would allow me to walk to classes independently. My parents and I visited HBU, in fact, during Open House week in the spring. I liked the small campus and the atmosphere. We had the chance to meet the University President, who said the school could work with me in meeting my academic needs. His assurance didn't stop concerns from creeping into my head.

How would I complete all of my college assignments? Would I really be able to manage by myself on campus?

I tried to push these worries out of my mind as I sat with my parents at the ARD. What I remembered most from that meeting, though, came from the speech pathologist, who had never met me.

"You're not what I expected. I'm quite impressed with your abilities."

***

I had mixed feelings about attending my high school graduation ceremony. While I wanted to celebrate my accomplishment with the class of 1991, I knew I would feel extremely nervous accepting my diploma on stage, whether I walked or was pushed in a wheelchair. Mom, Dad, and I felt worn out and frustrated with all that had happened to get me to this point. I did not need a ceremony on stage to celebrate my academic accomplishment. I had the diploma and the gold tassels to prove it.

I really did not end up making the decision not to participate in graduation. That weekend, my family went to a wedding in Dallas in which my sister was a bridesmaid. We had a great time. Dad and I shared a dance at the reception. My almost five foot frame barely reached the middle of his chest.

As I watched the happy couple celebrate the beginning of their future together, I wondered what my future held. My difficulties in high school ended. What difficulties would I encounter in pursuing my dreams?

I tried to look forward to summer in Palm Beach before thinking about college.

5

An Unexpected Death: Succumbing to Grief, Surviving

I became a vocational rehabilitation client for the first time in the fall of 1991. Before I came home from Florida, Mom called Texas Rehabilitation Commission (TRC) and received general information about assistance I could receive in attending college and obtaining employment. Since I was the client, I needed to make all future calls myself. This new responsibility challenged me physically and psychologically. I had to work on making my speech intelligible over the phone to people who never met me. I also needed to learn how to speak for myself instead of relying on my parents to advocate for me.

Dad brought me to the initial meeting scheduled with the counselor. Ms. Gibson and I discussed my goals and my interests in computers, as well as my abilities and disabilities. I showed her my high school transcript, and we briefly talked about my pursuing a college education. Before I began receiving any services, though, I went for a physical exam and a psychological evaluation.

My mom took me for a physical from a doctor we selected from TRC's list. The doctor briefly examined me and asked me some basic questions about my physical abilities, such as how many pounds I could lift and how far I could walk. A medical student stood in the room and observed. When the doctor asked me to do things I couldn't do (standing and touching my toes), the physician scribbled some notes on a form and ended the appointment.

For the psychological evaluation, Dad drove Nana and me to the assessment. Nana stayed with me because the testing took most of three days and I required assistance with lunch and breaks. Over those few days, a psychologist assessed my physical and intellectual skills, as well as my psychological state. She taped paper to the table and asked me to write my name, which embarrassed me because of its large size and sloppiness. I completed reading and math tests, and answered many questions recalling sequences of numbers and words. One test required me to close my eyes and touch different parts of my face with fingers on both hands. I remember laughing somewhat uncontrollably as I often did when I became nervous or uncomfortable with my inability to do what was asked. The psychologist and I talked about my difficulties in high school and my hopes for what I might accomplish in the future.

***

At home, I worked on our first personal computer my dad bought. Looking back, I find it difficult to believe that Dad didn't have a home computer sooner. Without the demands of school keeping me, or rather us, busy, he and I had time to experiment with computer hardware to determine which worked best for me.

Since I did not have the ability to use a typical mouse, he took me to a computer store to try other devices. I best used a trackball on which I only had to move the large ball to control the cursor onscreen. Two oversized buttons allowed me to click and double click icons. Using the trackball required practice. The first time Dad had me try our new hardware at home, I knocked the trackball over and the ball rolled across on the carpet! Mom stopped it before Dad saw what I did. Observing me as I tried to use the new system, he soon put Velcro on the back of the keyboard and the trackball, as well as the surface of the workstation, to stabilize everything and prevent any more hardware from flying.

***

Weeks later, I received a copy of the psychologist's report sent to Ms. Gibson. A listing and explanation of my high scores on the cognitive parts comprised most of the report. The report detailed my physical impairments and described the activities I could not do. She mentioned my uncontrollable laughter during that one test. The psychologist then stated the psychological difficulties she felt I experienced with adjusting to life away from the busy school environment. She felt that I may have had dysthymia, or mild depression. In conclusion, she recommended psychotherapy to help me cope with life after high school. While I certainly felt anxious about my future, reading her comments bothered me. Didn't most high school graduates, with or without disabilities, experience anxieties and doubts about their futures? Wasn't I allowed to experience these feelings, given my situation, and find my own ways to cope with them?

If I had the evaluation a few months later, I can only imagine what the report might have concluded about my psychological state. I soon experienced more sadness, anxiety, and uncertainty about my future than during any other time in my eighteen years.

***

The months leading up to and following the new year of 1992 were supposed to be an exciting time for the Torreno family. Cris graduated from college in December and became engaged that past summer. She and her fiancée Chad planned a May wedding. I anticipated their celebration and looked forward to starting college.

After celebrating Thanksgiving in San Antonio with our cousins, Mom, Dad, Nana and I watched Cris receive her degree from Texas A&M a few weeks later. Chad, who received his degree two years earlier, joined us, too. Following the ceremony, we enjoyed an Italian dinner at a College Station restaurant. My dad made a brief speech to congratulate his older daughter and then started crying. Cris rose from the table and hugged him. Although Dad rarely showed such emotion (I don't recall seeing him cry before that day), none of us thought much about his tears or the feelings behind them.

Days after a quiet Christmas, the four of us went to order Cris and Chad's wedding invitations. The details of the wedding were finalized, put in print and then mailed to family and friends. I saw the excitement in my sister's face as these preparations for her big day became real.

Our house grew quieter when Cris flew to Corpus Christi to visit Chad. Mom, Dad, Nana, and I didn't do much to ring in the new year, aside from eating black-eyed peas. I looked at the many opened gifts under the Christmas tree once again before bringing them to the room that I shared with Nana. The next day, I planned to type thank-you notes to out-of-town relatives who sent me gifts.

On Thursday, January 2nd, Dad picked up Cris at the airport and took her to lunch. Mom went out to run errands. Nana and I hung out together at home. For the first time in four and a half years, I realized I would not be an "only child" at home; my sister would live with us and work in Houston until her May wedding.

After Dad and Cris arrived home, he mentioned something about going to run errands. I heard him talking to Cris. As I saw him pass the living room, I said, "Oh, Dad, would you get my typewriter down? I need to write some thank-you notes."

He lifted the typewriter from the closet shelf next to my parents' bedroom. Then, he placed it on the game table and pushed the chair in with me sitting in it.

"Thanks."

"Okay, Stephanie. I love you," he said before kissing me.

After saying goodbye to Nana, who sat at the kitchen table, he left through the front door. Looking back, I don't remember if I told Dad I loved him. I did not know that conveying that sentiment at that moment would matter so much – and remain in my thoughts.

Afternoon turned into evening. Mom came home and we prepared to sit down to eat dinner.

"Where's your father?" she asked.

"I don't know," I said.

"Maybe he went to buy a new VCR," Cris suggested.

Eating dinner without Dad wasn't unusual. Mom and Nana liked to have dinner early, as did I before I felt too tired. On work days, Dad often came home between 6:30 and 7:00. Sometimes he came later, having lost track of time. Or, he ate, helped me with homework when I was in school, walked the dogs, and then returned to work to supervise the night crew. With these crazy hours, my mom joked that he should sleep in his office.

We still didn't worry too much by the next morning. Mom and Cris carried on with their plans to go look at bridesmaids' dresses. Nana and I went along to share the experience. I had already decided I didn't want to have to stand through the ceremony on the altar. I felt perfectly content as a member of the house party. Looking at all of the dresses was fun, though, and we went out to lunch afterwards. As Mom pulled into our driveway, we expected to see Dad's car in front of Cris' bedroom window. We didn't.

Cris called his office first. When no one answered, we began to think of whom to call next. My dad didn't really have any friends outside of work. He actively participated in our church and sang in the choir, but didn't have much time for social activities. Dad was extremely close to Terry, his cousin who was more like a sister to him. Mom called San Antonio to ask her if she saw or heard from him.

When she said she had not, I remember being startled when I heard Mom say, "Manolo is missing."

Hours passed slowly. My mom didn't know what to do. We took turns calling his office again. No answer. Finally, Cris called the police since more than twenty-four hours had passed. Before filing a missing person report, police suggested we call the county jail, the hospitals, the morgue. My sister did that. A forty-eight year old Hispanic male hadn't been seen in any of those places.

Day became night. More phone calls were made. Mom called Mrs. Grothaus, MaryLou to me now, our good friend and my former speech pathologist who lived a block from us. Over and over, I heard halves of hurried and tense conversations. My dad was missing and no one had seen him.

Nana started helping me get ready for bed. I couldn't concentrate on what I was doing. When Nana helped me wash my face and brush my teeth, my pajama top became soaking wet. She did not want me to go to bed like that, so she helped me change. Going to bed, I saw our Bichon Frise, Dolly, looking out the front window, waiting for Dad to come home. All of us waited. Where could he be? Did he get mugged somewhere? Was he lying on a street, hurt?

Morning finally came. After a sleepless night, we ate breakfast. Cris decided to take a shower, and I aimlessly walked around the kitchen in my mismatched pajamas. The phone rang. Mom picked it up. She began answering questions with "yes" and "no" responses. She began crying and almost dropped the phone, saying something about Dad was dead. Mom told me to go get Cris.

I ran as best I could into the steamy bathroom. Opening the second door to the tiny room with the commode and shower, I cut Cris off before she finished griping at me for invading her privacy.

"Dad's dead. Get out of the shower," I struggled to get the words out as I cried.

My dad's body was found by a security guard by the duck pond at Texas Instruments. He had shot himself. In the empty parking lot, his car contained the Bible in the front seat and a note that simply read, "Call my family" with our phone number. Dad wrote the note on paper from a local motel, one of two where he stayed. We also learned that he purchased the gun from a pawn shop. Receipts from the motels and the store found in his briefcase showed his barely recognizable signature.

I remember having to dress, but I couldn't pick something to wear. Nana helped me. I could hear Mom making phone call after phone call. MaryLou came over immediately. Terry and Joe started driving from San Antonio with their daughter Laurie. Laurie's three brothers began the trip as well.

MaryLou left when our priest came to our house. In our living room, Father Ed sat with Mom, Cris, and me and talked about what happened. I can't remember anything specific said. We prayed. Cris reminded Father Ed that she and Dad saw him at the restaurant where they ate lunch on Thursday. She asked Father Ed if he sensed anything different about Dad. He didn't.

The doorbell rang many times in the following hours. Each time I regained my composure, another neighbor or friend came to pay their respects, and I lost it again in a flood of tears. Chad came. Terry, Joe, and Laurie arrived. We tried to piece together the last few weeks of Dad's life. Yes, he seemed quiet, but he was always quiet. He remained somewhat of a loner. Maybe he drank more than usual in recent months, but he never got drunk.

Terry then mentioned receiving two phone calls the day before in which the caller didn't say anything. She felt and heard someone on the other end of the line. My dad's beloved cousin spoke his name, but still no response came. All of us were convinced Dad couldn't say anything on the other end of the line.

That night, Cris and I sat on Mom and Dad's bed, wiping each other's tears. We talked about everything, including practical matters. Dad - a husband, a father, a friend, and our primary breadwinner – was gone. I lost an advocate. We could not afford to stay in our house. Cris and I volunteered to return some of our Christmas presents. Mom didn't want us to do that, but much of our lives would change. Cris and Chad's wedding would likely need to be postponed. Mom held my hand. I told her I loved her and that I would do anything to help her.

"You especially needed both of us," she said to me.

We all needed him.

6
Trying to Move Forward: Mourning, Celebrating

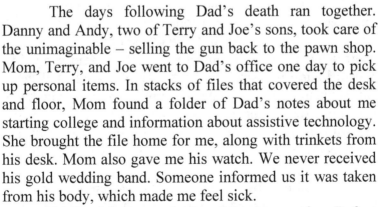

The days following Dad's death ran together. Danny and Andy, two of Terry and Joe's sons, took care of the unimaginable – selling the gun back to the pawn shop. Mom, Terry, and Joe went to Dad's office one day to pick up personal items. In stacks of files that covered the desk and floor, Mom found a folder of Dad's notes about me starting college and information about assistive technology. She brought the file home for me, along with trinkets from his desk. Mom also gave me his watch. We never received his gold wedding band. Someone informed us it was taken from his body, which made me feel sick.

Dad's visitation took place Monday evening. Before other family and friends came, Mom and Cris walked with me to see Dad's body in the open casket. Except for the way his hair was combed, he looked like Dad. He looked peaceful. I touched his hand, which felt cold and caused me to shiver. I told him I loved him. Walking back to the foyer, I saw teachers from middle school – Mrs. Stamm, Miss Foley. I didn't want anyone who hugged me to let go. I saw many more familiar faces, and just as many from Texas Instruments that I didn't know.

My dad's funeral mass was held on Tuesday, January 7th. In her bathroom, Mom put make-up on me. She tried to, rather. I could not look at her without tears starting to run down my cheeks. She took my hand.

"You need to try to keep it together today. Dad would want that. Go slowly and try to do your best walking."

My black dress shoes didn't allow me to walk with my arms by my side in a relaxed manner. Still, Mom's advice gave me something to concentrate on as we walked into church. Mom wanted me to sit in the first pew before she, Cris, Chad, and Nana joined me. I felt relieved to rest my legs, though I didn't like sitting alone. As people filled into church, I glanced and tried to smile at those I recognized. I then felt an arm around my shoulder. Stacy, Cris' college roommate and her future maid of honor, came to sit with me. Her presence comforted me.

I remember hearing some of the beautiful music the choir sang, though I cannot recall any specific song. My cousin Laurie has since told me that "On Eagle's Wings" was sung and Terry becomes emotional each time she hears it. I don't remember hearing it, so the song still comforts me with memories of my father. As Miss Foley returned from receiving Communion, she came over to me in a red trimmed black dress.

"You're showing a bit of cleavage, aren't you?" she whispered before I giggled and hugged her.

The end of the funeral mass brought brief distraction as my family walked to the lobby to thank friends for coming. An assistant principal I befriended in high school wanted to get me a chair. I politely refused; standing and balancing on my feet gave me something to do. My former neurologist complimented my walking to Mom. I felt relieved that my physical balance held me when everything else seemed so off kilter.

We invited out-of-town family and friends to our house after the funeral. Plenty of food had been brought over those three days. Pat and Charlie, who took care of Cris and me when we lived in Dallas, made my lunch. After we ate, Charlie and I sat together at the computer as he showed me how to play some games. Mom told me later that she heard me laugh a little as she and Pat, a former biology professor, talked about what an autopsy may or may not reveal about Dad's suicide.

Before Pat and Charlie left, she asked when I was going to start college. I told her I did not have any idea. She wanted me to think about applying to the university outside of Dallas where she worked as an administrator. Pat told me I would receive as much assistance as I needed. I know she meant well and wanted the best future for me, but I did not want to contemplate leaving Mom.

My dad's ashes were buried between his parents' graves that Saturday in San Antonio. Mom, Cris, and I sat in the car when the funeral director brought out the simple wooden rectangular box and placed it in the back seat next to me. Cris joked with me about sitting next to "Dad." I had a difficult time believing the contents in that box were my father's body.

A few friends from Houston came to mourn with us at the graveside service. Since Dad grew up and went to college as an undergraduate in San Antonio, people who had known him were present. Catholic priests and brothers attended. I later heard that some of these men who taught

Dad were not surprised that he took his own life. After his mother's death when my dad was eighteen, and his father's death before my parents married, they worried about his depression and despondency.

The evening we arrived home, MaryLou invited us to dinner at her house. I felt tired, yet I didn't want to go home. I did not know what would happen over the next few weeks and months. The shock of the past ten days had not worn off. I do not remember when it did. I only knew the services ended, the flowers people sent died, and life changed forever. As I saw Dolly looking out the front window every night for weeks, waiting for her master to come home and take her for a walk, I imagined hearing Dad coming home. I knew I wouldn't hear the click of the lock, though.

The business of Dad's death consumed my mom's time before and after she went back to work two weeks later. Mom needed to hire a lawyer. Dad's outdated and out-of-state will, found in his dresser, would not be used. Chad's parents sold Dad's car after we cleaned out piles of paperwork in the trunk. Our boat kept in Galveston was sold, but not before Mom applied for a new title to replace the one we couldn't find. Finances worried us constantly. Would we be able to stay in our house until Mom sold it? Would Dad's modest life insurance policy pay in the case of suicide?

A human resources employee from TI, who lived in our neighborhood, came to our house to assist Mom in completing paperwork. Dad gave Mr. Burgess a ride to work a few times while I was in high school. Now, he helped us. Mom and I continued coverage under Dad's medical insurance policy for eighteen months. We received Dad's pay for vacation days he didn't take. With the life insurance claim filed, we waited to find out if we would receive it.

After they finished the paperwork, Mr. Burgess told Mom that the pressure on employees at TI was relentless.

***

Nana dropped me off at Heflin one day to see the school counselor, who taught me in fifth grade. I visited Mom, now the assistant librarian, and then spent an hour with Mrs. Thompson. We talked about the myriad of emotions I felt. When I felt angry, she recommended scribbling on sheets of newspaper. I never did that; I didn't think we had enough newspapers to release the anger I felt. I told her I continued to read books that friends brought us about dealing with suicide. One book explained that an individual "completes suicide," rather than "commits suicide," since killing oneself is not a crime. I disagreed. My dad's act felt like he committed a crime, and Mom, Cris, and I were being punished.

During the next couple of weeks, former teachers started calling and taking me to different places. Cindy Foley took me to Dave and Buster's to play the arcades. We hung out at her apartment. Mrs. Jones, the PE assistant who helped me at Heflin, brought me to her son's football games at Hastings. I enjoyed the temporary distractions. At a basketball game between Hastings and our chief rival, I had a chance to talk to Mr. Lowery, now an assistant principal. I didn't know he came to my father's viewing until he told me.

"I now know you were right, Mr. Lowery. Life is unfair."

"Yes, Stephanie, but the rest of the quote, however, involves overcoming obstacles."

With Mom and Cris at work, I started finding obstacles to overcome. Small ones, one at a time. Spending days at home with Nana, who seemed oblivious to what we were experiencing, I tackled whatever needed doing. Nana helped in her own way, but she and my father never liked each other. As a result, she offered little support, particularly to my mom, during those most difficult months. Nana didn't want Mom to sell our home. We needed to move eventually, and Mom and I wanted a new start. Staying busy helped me avoid thinking too much, so I began cleaning out closets, drawers, whatever I could do and whatever I could try to do to help Mom. Mom showed me how to do laundry, which I learned to do without spilling too much powdered detergent. My new goal became figuring out how to do, or at least try to do, chores around the house that no one, including myself, thought I could do.

***

A few weeks after Dad died, Mom took me to a meeting with my vocational rehabilitation counselor. Ms. Gibson expressed shock when we told her of Dad's death. Reviewing my psychological report, the counselor asked me where I wanted to go to college and mentioned an out-of-town university that provided good support services. Although I realized I needed to think about my future, attending college didn't seem possible - financially, physically, or emotionally.

I just lost Dad; how could I possibly choose to leave Mom? I told her I wanted to put my college plans on hold. My new goal included trying to enter a program for adults with disabilities called Project Independence. Offered at the central campus of Houston Community College, Project Independence was a year-long computer class offering students college credit. Applicants had to pass an entrance exam and interview with a business advisory council. Toward the end of the program, students completed an internship and, hopefully, gained employment. The counselor accepted my change of plans. Another Project Independence class would not begin for many months. My counselor found more information about the program and kept me informed about the application process. Working toward this new goal diminished my fear of leaving home to attend college.

***

Most of the arrangements scheduled for my Cris' May wedding were postponed. My sister's wedding took place August 22nd, which would have been, coincidently, Daddy George's seventy-ninth birthday. By the spring, I began working on my primary contribution to the wedding by inputting guests' names and addresses into two word processing files (for inside and outside envelopes) to take to the printers. A neighbor showed me how to format the files correctly. My lack of speed kept me busy and my mind somewhat occupied. At a bridal shower given in my sister's college sorority house, we saw Terry, Laurie, and Joe, who drove from San Antonio. Before Joe left the house during the shower, Cris asked ask our "uncle" to walk her down the aisle. Her crying after he agreed to the honor illustrated the constant mix of emotions all of us experienced.

That summer before the wedding, I decided not to go with Nana to Palm Beach. I did not want to leave Mom. She had so much to do with both matters of Dad's death and Cris and Chad's wedding. I wanted and needed to support her in any way I could, so Nana went to Florida alone for a few weeks. With Cris working and visiting Chad out of town, Mom and I continued to clean out closets and prepared to put the house on the market. We established new routines. She walked Dolly and her doggy daughter, Nanette, while I walked or rode my large tricycle, something I did when Dad worked in the yard.

Nana's seventy-seventh birthday on August 20th marked the beginning of four days of wedding celebrations. At a pre-rehearsal cocktail party (given by the Blizzards – our friends from Heflin), the rehearsal dinner, and the bridesmaids' luncheon, I enjoyed seeing friends and family, some of whom I hadn't seen – or remembered - since our move to Texas. Nancy, Mom's cousin, came from upstate New York, as did Barbara and Greg, my sister's godparents. At nineteen, I felt I was meeting them for the first time. These few days helped me forge long distance relationships that continue today.

The big evening finally came. In the late afternoon, a limousine pulled up in front of our house to take us to church. Mom, Nana, and I wore our dresses, while Cris wore a jumpsuit after having her hair done and applying her make-up. At church, I watched as Cris' bridesmaids and the wedding coordinator helped her with her gown. Escorted by one of the ushers, I walked down the aisle before the grandparents, Chad's parents, and Mom. My long, pale pink dress hid most of my feet in my matching flats. I relaxed a bit when the usher held my hand with his arm in mine. I again found myself sitting alone until Nana and Mom were seated. I thought about Dad's funeral seven months earlier. Cris, no doubt, felt the same mixture of emotions as she briefly broke into tears during the ceremony.

The photographer took pictures of both families and the wedding party. I noticed friends stayed in the back of the church to watch. After the pictures were taken, I went to talk to Pat and Charlie. Since they had misplaced the directions to the reception, I told them I would go with them. I enjoyed the chance to talk to them. I updated Pat and Charlie with my plans to try to move forward. Pat still wanted me to consider attending college outside Dallas. My new goal, I told her, involved trying to get into Project Independence. I wasn't abandoning the hope of pursuing a college degree, however, I did not want to do it at that time. As Charlie pulled into the parking garage of the reception, I felt relieved that our topic of conversation changed to the celebration of the newlyweds. On the way into the club, Pat and Charlie squabbled at each other as they saw my difficulties in keeping up with their quick strides.

That night was the latest I ever stayed up, as Mom, Nana, and I went home at about 1:00 in the morning. We did not sleep much because, on Sunday morning, Chad's parents hosted a brunch to send the couple off on their honeymoon. We visited Nancy and others who traveled far to be with us one last time. The celebrations ended and real life began again.

***

Soon after the wedding, Mom drove me downtown to the central campus of Houston Community College to take the exam for Project Independence. I worried about working with a scribe, but a college student who wrote my answers and bubbled in the scantron sheet assisted me really well. He asked me how I did so many calculations in my head. With years of practice, I explained, I didn't know any different.

The next step toward Project Independence included an interview with members of the Business Advisory Council, computer professionals who guided the program's curriculum. This part made me most nervous. I know not many people enjoy interviews, but nervousness causes my CP to go haywire. My muscles tighten, my speech becomes harder to produce, and therefore understand, and I sweat to the point of visibility. Trying to control these obvious difficulties - and I do try - I forget exactly how I want to say what I'm thinking. I knew I needed to do my best, though.

The interview took place in one of the classrooms where the class met. To my surprise, Ms. Gibson, my vocational rehabilitation counselor, sat in the back of the room. Five men and women in business clothes sat in the front row. I sat down in front of them, discreetly smoothing my skirt and attempting to relax. They introduced themselves and began asking questions. One read from my file and reported that I did well on the exam. My sudden burst of confidence ended quickly though, when one of the women asked me, "What will you do if you are not accepted into Project Independence?"

"I guess I will start college. I really want to concentrate on learning about computers." What could I say? I lied, and I sounded convincing.

With that answer, the interviewers asked me to take a break. Ms. Gibson walked over to me, and we left the room together. She told me how well I had done. A few minutes later, one of the BAC members asked us back into the room. I sat down again.

"Congratulations, Stephanie. You are one of the youngest students we have ever accepted into Project Independence."

***

With the program's start months away, Mom and I became anxious for our house to sell. If I planned on taking MetroLift, the paratransit system for the disabled, to go back and forth to school, we needed to live within specific boundaries of the city. Mom already knew where she wanted to live. We kept passing two townhome complexes on both sides on the same street. Mom always liked the townhomes since we lived in Houston, and wanted us to think about moving when Dad was still alive. He didn't want to move. Now, had to move, but our house had to sell first.

Our house had been for sale since the spring after Dad died. Potential buyers came during showing after showing, but all they did was look. Showings became a hassle because our little, ferocious dogs had to go outside and everything needed to look nice. I remember shoving things in drawers as the doorbell rang.

Finally, a potential buyer looked at the house again. I sat in the backyard when she looked at the house a second time. Mom wasn't home, so her realtor and she started asking me questions about the plants and trees. I tried to recall the names of everything my dad planted, though I had little idea what I was saying. Our backyard, with a two-seater bench swing hanging from the wood patio cover, was my favorite place. I tried to sell it on that alone, truthfully sharing with the woman that my sister got engaged on that bench. Sentiment sells!

The woman made an offer, albeit a low one. Mom and I worried about what the home inspection might reveal. The day of the inspection, for example, heavy rain accumulated in the atrium, with water rising above the mud and plants to the frame of the sliding glass door. It did not look good. We wish we knew then that the drain there, but it was covered under mud. After a neighbor told us to poke around for it, Mom went out with a rake, slashing thick mud all around the enclosed area. She relieved lots of anger and stress with every maneuver.

Our house finally sold in the spring. We looked at townhomes for months, and now Mom could make an offer on one with three bedrooms. The townhouse would be my first two-story home. Mom and I discussed having a stair lift installed, but I first wanted to see how I did without one. Show my mom that all of those years of PT paid off! The carpeted stairs boosted my confidence in climbing up and down.

After months and months of struggling with so many emotions and keeping busy, we moved. Nana reluctantly went along; she helped me again tremendously when I began Project Independence. Although we donated or sold furniture and many other items, so much that we took kept movers going in and out of the house where I grew up. On one last trip, the movers discovered some clutter in the attic above the garage. A toy chest - a round, yellow elephant with brightly colored polka dots on it - came down. The whimsical plastic chest, still containing old toys, went to the curb for whomever to find. Seeing that toy chest in front of the house as Mom drove away, I knew I was no longer a child, whether I felt like an adult or not.

7
Returning to School:
A New Beginning, The
Same Struggle

Just a week or two after our move, Project Independence began in the steamy June heat of 1993. Nana decided that she did not want me to take MetroLift, so she drove me back and forth to class, which I appreciated. I found the lack of air conditioning in her car uncomfortable, however, during the forty minute ride, especially on the way home. The program started gradually, with three hours of instruction, before meeting a full day until late afternoon.

Since class first met in the morning only, it did not make sense for Nana to drive home and back again within three hours. So, she joined the class, which included three other students, with me being the one female student at first. My instincts soon confirmed that Nana didn't belong in my classroom. She convinced herself she understood Mr. Hamlin's lectures introducing us to computer science, when in fact, she didn't. Her lack of understanding the material, however, did not stop my outspoken grandmother from attempting to answer questions, or encouraging me to do so. I wanted and needed to prove my independence in class, and Nana's presence and endless chatter prevented me from doing that.

Around the time class began meeting full days, the building's air conditioning broke. Several fans provided us with some air, but learning in the classroom, dressed in required business casual clothes, did not work for me. The energy I used to simply sit in the extremely warm environment drained me. My entire body broke out in a full-blown sweat walking to and from the restroom. After a day or two of trying to hide my discomfort, I told Mr. Hamlin that I did not feel well and could not eat my lunch, let alone make it through the afternoon. My tendency to become overheated kept class from meeting all day until the air conditioning was repaired. As relieved as I felt to leave at noon for the equally hot ride home, I found myself shaking my head - more than normal - at Nana's annoying attempts to become a computer science student.

When class finally extended to six to seven hours, depending on the day, I knew Nana's absence would force me to manage my needs independently. From the first day of class, I realized I was the most physically challenged student. Lloyd, who may have been in his fifties, walked with a cane. He also had diabetes, as I saw him giving himself insulin shots at lunch. Terry, another middle-aged man, had a hidden disability. Alan, a young man around my age, wore leg braces and used metal crutches. Jane, who joined our group a few weeks into class, was in her thirties.

After getting to know each other, she told me she had depression. Unlike my four classmates, I had difficulties with most activities and required additional time to do what they did easily. Although the program met all students' needs, I knew if I wanted to become more employable, I needed to increase my independence inside and outside class.

As I already knew, using a public restroom includes many more difficulties than using the bathroom at home. Obviously, having the ability to open the restroom door is necessary. My ninety-pound frame struggled to push the heavy door, and my compromised balance felt like it could give way at any minute. After getting in the door, I eventually learned how to lock the stall door. Often, I can do something almost perfectly one time, and have difficulties doing the same task later. When I couldn't lock the door, I closed it and hoped no one barged in. Although I found the grab bars helpful in the wheelchair-accessible stall, the higher commode left my feet dangling, which never helps my balance. Washing my hands did not cause too many challenges, but water on the floor always posed a hazard. Pulling the door open to leave was harder and scarier since I didn't want to be hit and knocked down.

I debated if I should mention these challenges to the director of the program. Project Independence, after all, represented an opportunity to demonstrate my abilities, not to highlight my obvious disabilities. A staff member, however, did it for me, suggesting I needed an assistant with me throughout the day. I decided that I did not want that, and I kept trying to manage on my own. Jane accompanied me to the restroom, or Terry opened the door with his head turned to avoid seeing or being seen inside.

Most of my peers went out to lunch. As the only student who couldn't drive, I stayed in the classroom and took my time opening and eating what Nana and Mom knew I could handle.

***

A few weeks into our long days of class, I felt very tired. I was not sleeping well. Most days, I found myself anxious over anything and everything. When I was not busy with school, which occupied most of my time, I thought about Dad's death, its circumstances, and its aftermath. I decided to talk to my doctor.

Dr. Hoyle had been my pediatrician since we moved to Houston. He examined me for the school district before I began second grade. Cris also saw him, and we immediately felt comfortable with him. Dr. Hoyle's gentle bedside manner and confidence in my progress and abilities eased some of the tension that always seemed to shadow me.

Nana drove to my appointment. Although Mom accompanied me into an examining room during my visits, I did not want Nana to join me. I saw Dr. Hoyle once since my dad's suicide. He did not know what happened and I needed to talk to him alone. My legs quivered and I tried to control my arm movements as Dr. Hoyle walked in and we started to talk.

I briefly told the doctor about Dad's death. Dr. Hoyle listened carefully as I described many of the changes that occurred since he died and my decisions about delaying college. I told him about Project Independence and my hope to gain employment after the program. I wanted and needed to feel better to do my best in school, but I realized my increasing anxiety and insomnia did not help.

"You can always go to college, especially if you are going to be President one day. What we need to do, though, is help you control some of this movement. I can give you something to help you relax at night, but you should only take it a few nights a week. Now, should I get my nurse to help you undress for your checkup?"

"No, Dr. Hoyle. I do not have time for a checkup today. I need to get to school."

"Okay, but we need to check your blood pressure again. It's too high."

The nurse came in again and reported my blood pressure remained elevated. Dr. Hoyle wanted me to come after school for a few days to keep checking it. So, on the way home, Nana took me by the office. I did not think sitting in afternoon traffic, hoping to arrive at the doctor's office before it closed, helped. After a week or two of going each afternoon, my blood pressure remained high.

Dr. Hoyle stopped to see me one afternoon and told me what I sensed, but did not want to hear. At twenty, I was becoming too old to be treated under his care, and I needed to have my hypertension diagnosed and treated. He talked to his colleagues, and he wanted me to see an internist in the same building.

Nana again drove me to my appointment with Dr. Adams, who ordered several tests. While she did not find any particular cause, the doctor said I probably had high blood pressure because of genetics – my mom had been diagnosed several years earlier. Dr. Adams put me on low dose medication. Another change I did not want.

Dr. Adams treated me, and my very reluctant and stubborn grandmother, for a couple of years. I never felt she and I connected as doctor and patient, particularly the next few times I saw her. Although I stopped to see Dr. Hoyle whenever I was in the building, and sometimes saw him other places, I knew I would not have another physician like him again.

***

The routine in class changed. After weeks of listening to lectures, we moved to the computer lab next door for hands-on experience. My physical differences stood out again as my classmates could use any PC in the room; I sat at the computer with the keyguard on the keyboard and the trackball by its side. I knew my equipment allowed me to keep pace as much as I could with everyone. Still, as Mr. Hamlin watched me type on that first day, he and Jyoti, the lab assistant, knew I needed more help.

"We're going to install StickyKeys on your computer."

I never heard of the software program. Soon, it became my favorite assistive technology feature. Well, maybe my second favorite feature – until a few years later. Rather than having to put my right hand on the keyguard and try to aim for and hold down the correct key, I tapped the Shift, Ctrl, or Alt key once, and it would "stick" until I typed another key. With StickyKeys, I truly became the one-handed typist, albeit a really slow one, I had been since first grade.

Once we finished practicing what we learned about DOS and understood word processing basics in WordPerfect, our class moved on to working in Windows. Understanding how to accomplish tasks with icons and menus came easily to me. Guiding the trackball still didn't work well for me, even with practice at home. When I eventually moved the cursor to where I wanted it, I could click and double-click an icon. Dragging something on the monitor wasn't going to happen by my hand, though. Fortunately, Mr. Hamlin and Jyoti had a solution for those difficulties. MouseKeys software gave me more precise control in clicking and dragging icons, allowing me to use the numeric keypad to move the pointer onscreen. The program was slow, though. I continued to use the trackball to move the pointer to the general area of where I wanted it. MouseKeys helped me avoid frustration when my arm and hand movements became too difficult to control. As with StickyKeys, MouseKeys has been an accessibility feature in Windows for years. Using the computer would pose frustrations and challenges if I did not have access to these programs.

As I grew more comfortable using the computer in class, I tried to focus less on my lack of speed. Along with MouseKeys, Mr. Hamlin taught me the keyboard alternatives so that I had many options to accomplish the same tasks. My intellectual abilities often helped me stay on track with classmates, or one step ahead of them. If I did not physically keep up with each instruction when we worked as a group, I remembered what to do and eventually caught up. I especially felt proud of myself when we learned Excel. One day after class, I heard our instructor say I figured out certain formulas before the other students did.

***

After almost a year in class, the time came to begin my internship. Our goal of entering the workplace and demonstrating our skills to employers might lead to permanent employment. Again, my inability to drive and my other disabilities limited my options. While Mr. Hamlin placed my classmates in positions quickly, my placement posed a challenge. A nonprofit organization that served individuals with hearing and speech impairments seemed interested in offering me an internship. Mr. Hamlin brought me to meet the staff and ask questions. At the end of the meeting, they did not offer me an opportunity.

The disappointment crushed me. Would I ever receive an opportunity to demonstrate my skills? Would any employer see past my limitations and acknowledge my motivation and ability to work? If I had this much difficulty finding work with Mr. Hamlin's assistance, what hope did I have looking for employment on my own?

My internship ended up allowing me to remain in the computer lab, working for one of the college administrators. Although I interviewed with Dr. Jepson and another administrator on a different campus, Dr. Jepson brought my work with him when he visited the central campus. This convenient arrangement worked well since I became accustomed to the environment, but I felt disappointed because I did not have a chance to experience the working world away from campus. No doubt a new workplace would have caused me challenges and anxieties. Still, I wondered what new experiences might bring. I enjoyed the fact that Jyoti continued working in the lab, too.

While working, I felt frustrated when Dr. Jepson gave work instructions to Jyoti, rather than to me directly. He knew I understood him, and he apparently understood my speech. After all, he interviewed me. With each visit, Dr. Jepson seemed too preoccupied to speak to me, the individual doing the actual work. Maybe he did not realize it. I obviously did, and unfortunately, continue to be aware of and annoyed by people who talk around me instead of to me. Along with earning my first paycheck, I earned insight into being an adult with a disability.

My computer skills, or "talents" as Joyti called them, led me to want to practice more at home. In the few years since Dad brought it home, however, our computer became obsolete. If I wanted to keep my skills current and continue improving my speed, I needed a new computer. Jyoti helped me advocate for a new computer from TRC. I not only wanted to teach myself more software applications, I also hoped to find some type of work to do at home. Jyoti taught me a new concept of sending electronic files from my home computer to one in the lab. I began to think of possibilities of putting my skills to work at home without having to be driven back and forth to a workplace.

I received a new computer around the time my internship ended. By then, my vocational rehabilitation case had been assigned to a new counselor when Ms.

Gibson left. My new counselor did not seem to understand my goals or know how to support me in finding telecommuting work. He sounded less than pleased when he called once and I informed him I was practicing my keyboarding skills by playing a game!

My goal seemed out of reach as summer arrived. I had little to do. Soon, life threw me off balance again. This time, I experienced an excruciatingly difficult period in which I seriously doubted if I could regain it – or even if I possessed the motivation to try.

8
Another Loss:
Grieving Again, Looking
Ahead

I don't remember how long I saw the raised, multicolored area of skin between Nana's breasts. In the summer, if she didn't pull the top of her bathing suit far enough, the bluish, purplish spot showed near her cleavage. I worried about it. We all worried about it. Mom thought it was skin cancer and kept trying to persuade Nana to go to a doctor. Each year, when Mom went for routine physicals and mammograms, she asked my grandmother if she wanted to go, too. Nana would not have any of it. She went to Mom's doctor once and he gave her samples of high blood pressure medication. A couple of pills were taken and the rest sat on the bathroom counter.

During the last few months of Project Independence, Nana complained of not feeling well. She drove me back and forth to school, but her energy seemed to be waning. My petite yet plump grandmother was losing weight. When Mom and I picked her up from the bus station after what would be her final trip to Palm Beach, Mom later mentioned to me that she didn't recognize her. In her black and white outfit, Nana looked gray.

An appointment I had with Dr. Adams finally convinced her to have a checkup. As I walked with Nana to Dr. Adams' waiting room, I stopped to see Dr. Hoyle in his office. I said a quick "hello" and told him that I never thought of my grandmother as elderly until then. Upstairs, I waited for Nana outside one of the examining rooms.

A few weeks later, Nana's near inability to move without pain forced Mom to call Dr. Adams, who could not discuss Nana's health without her permission. Sitting on an upholstered chair in the living room, Nana shouted "yes" to give consent to the doctor as Mom held the phone in the air. I heard my mom's voice change with the few words she spoke as she listened to Dr. Adams.

The doctor thought Nana had breast cancer. The cancer most likely had spread.

When Mom hung up the phone, she sat down and told us the physician's recommendations. In between tears of sadness and anger, Mom said we needed to find Nana an oncologist and a surgeon. Nana immediately made it clear that she did not want surgery, which, as it turned out, would not have helped since the cancer had spread. Since Dr. Adams only saw patients at a hospital in Houston's medical center, which was far from our townhouse, Mom put in a call to Dr. Ericson, who practiced at a hospital ten minutes from home.

That night, as the three of us sat and tried to watch television, Nana made the dramatic statement, "I think I'm going to have to go into the hospital."

I suddenly lost it. As I tried to control the tears that I felt drown me, I ran to the stairs. I made it to the third or fourth step when I flopped down and started sobbing. I wanted to go upstairs and be alone. I was angry - at everyone and everything. Why was all of this happening now? Why did Dad die, and why was Nana probably going to die soon, too? Why was everyone I loved leaving me?

Mom prevented me from going to my room. She came to the stairs, held me, and finally walked me back to the living room.

"See what you're doing to your granddaughter. If you went for checkups and mammograms with me, maybe this wouldn't have happened. It may have been caught early and treated."

With my emotions overwhelming me, I decided to try to stop feeling them. Mom didn't need to deal with my emotions, too. I tried not to feel anything, attempting to make it through a day without sadness, anger, or confusion. I wanted to help Mom and Nana without letting anything bother me. I hoped a sense of emotional numbness would soon take over me.

I learned shortly that my plan did not work – and had lasting effects.

***

Emotional numbness did not come. Instead, I started feeling a sickening knot in my stomach when I woke up each morning. I felt better after I ate, but the ache stayed with me. Mom thought I was developing an ulcer; she had one in college and had to be hospitalized. She warned me about letting my anxiety control me and kept advising me to calm down. Of course, she knew from experience that "calming down" was something to say, but difficult to do.

I felt worse thinking about Mom having to deal with me in addition to figuring out what to do for Nana. At summer's end, Mom left her elementary school registrar position, which she held for two stressful years. She wanted to do something new. Her next job involved more stress - taking care of her mother and her daughter simultaneously. Nana's retirement income helped support us.

The jumpy, queasy feeling in my stomach made us go to the doctor. Dr. Adams listened as I described my symptoms, but she did not understand all of what I said. Mom filled in the details. The doctor then said something that surprised me.

"I think you're depressed."

Why did Dr. Adams' diagnosis surprise me? I guess just hearing the word 'depressed' made me feel weak. I knew I felt depressed. I did not, however, understand what depression meant yet. When the doctor suggested medication, I became adamant in my desire to fight it without pills.

"I want to try to feel better on my own."

Dr. Adams prescribed an over-the-counter medication to aid my sick stomach. I rationalized that easing my achy stomach would allow me to gain control over my psychological pain. Weeks would pass, and I became more lost in my head before I realized depression wasn't something to fight without treatment. My dad's death should have taught me that lesson.

***

Nana was right; she did need to go into the hospital. By the time Mom scheduled an appointment with a surgeon, as per recommendation, Nana could barely move. Instead of Mom bringing her to the surgeon, an ambulance brought my grandmother to the emergency room. The surgeon met us there, and admitted Nana for the month of October. Even if she agreed to surgery, it would not have changed the fact that the tumor, which started in one breast and erupted between her cleavage, spread to her bones. Nana's ribs hurt the most. During her hospital stay, she began taking Tamoxifin, an oral form of chemotherapy, and received radiation. She also received physical therapy. As Mom and I talked to the surgeon, I blurted out the question on my mind.

"How long does she have to live?"

Insane question. He, of course, did not have an answer. Mom could not believe I asked. I could not either, but I wanted to be prepared.

Our townhouse needed to accommodate Nana's changing needs. She couldn't climb stairs anymore, and without a bedroom downstairs, Mom ordered a hospital bed for our living room. While our dining room was nearest to the bathroom, the living room had more space and allowed Nana to watch TV with us. Nana's bed, against the mirrored wall on the far side of the living room, remained a fixture for over two years.

Once Nana came home, a new routine developed – a difficult one. Mom helped her dress and made her wear flat shoes. She was picked up by a hospital van for outpatient radiation a few times a week. When she didn't go for treatment, Nana sat in the peachy pink upholstered chair ten steps from her bed. She did everything from that chair – ate there, watched TV there, napped there. Mom served her food on a tray, since our kitchen chairs felt too hard for her to sit. The Asian garden stool between the matching chairs served as her table. Walking the hallway to the bathroom became her daily exercise between visits from a physical therapist. Although she could have had a home health aide come a few times per week, she did not want one. Mom and I shared the job.

I quickly learned how challenging caregiving, especially for an elderly loved one, can become. I felt obligated to – and really wanted to - give back some of the care Nana always gave me. As I tried to help as much as I physically could, I felt I was losing myself at twenty-two.

***

I remember reading or hearing somewhere that not all individuals with depression cry. My experience with depression made me cry all of the time, and I felt like I never stopped. When I wasn't crying, I tried to concentrate on anything that would occupy my mind. I could not. Mom and I made the decision to call Dr. Adams and ask her to prescribe an anti-depressant.

Anti-depressants take a few weeks to work, as Dr. Adams advised us. After taking the first few doses, however, I experienced extreme nervousness – to the point of trembling. I became used to feeling nervous. This feeling, however, differed from my usual anxiety. As I told Mom, I felt as if all I could do was sit in a corner and quiver. I had enough difficulty with involuntary movements; I could not imagine living through days while my body learned to tolerate this side effect. Thinking about how I appeared, with my limbs flailing more than ever, I cried to Mom.

"I don't want you to see me like this."

"It's okay. I know you're hurting. I don't mind."

"I do. You have enough to deal with right now."

I felt more helpless than ever. Mom called the doctor again, who prescribed another medication. After another few doses, I felt similar side effects. By the third or fourth call, and with the third or fourth prescription, Dr. Adams told Mom I needed to see a psychiatrist.

Mom had to find another doctor quickly; this time, for me. Since I needed to begin seeing a psychiatrist regularly, Mom asked Dr. Ericson for a recommendation close to home. She called the psychiatrist and made the earliest appointment available. In the meantime, Mom took me on short outings and tried to encourage me to talk. I barely spoke. Even if I wanted to, I did not know how to express what I felt.

"Stephanie, you're going to have to talk to someone. If it can't be me, you're going to have to talk to this psychiatrist."

***

Cris came to see us for a weekend from Austin, where she and Chad lived while my brother-in-law earned his MBA. My sister slept on the trundle bed in my room. We talked a little, but I didn't know what to say or how to ask her if she ever experienced the awful feelings I felt. Her life seemed to be moving on; mine seemed to be going nowhere, except toward more pain. That Sunday, when she and Mom went out to breakfast, I stayed home with Nana. I felt too nervous to go out in public.

The next Monday, Mom and I sat in the psychiatrist's waiting room. We saw him through the sliding glass window, discussing something with the receptionist. He looked annoyed.

He came out with his shirt sleeves rolled up. Mom introduced both of us.

"I'm Dr. Levine. I'm sorry, but there's been a mix-up. Stephanie is scheduled for next Monday. I can't see her today because I have a meeting."

Mom was angry. I just sat there, lost in my head, wondering what had happened that landed me in this office. Why couldn't I just feel like me again? Did I even remember what I felt like when I was me?

Dr. Levine again confirmed I had an appointment a week later.

Without the extreme shakiness from the pills I wasn't taking, I tried to concentrate on keeping busy the next seven days. I sat in front of the computer, attempting to type mailing labels to help Mom update her address book. My left thumb hit the keys, but my thoughts drifted elsewhere. I kept trying to focus on the monitor, which became blurry as tears welled up in my eyes.

Mom and I sat in the same waiting room one week later. I continued to feel anxious. This time, I became anxious just thinking about revealing my private thoughts and emotions to a stranger. What if he didn't understand my speech? How could he help me? When would I feel better? What if I never felt like myself, whomever she was, again? What if he thought I was crazy?

Dr. Levine opened the door and led us into his office. Mom and I already decided she would go in with me. I didn't want to be alone during the first meeting, and I didn't think I could tell him everything I needed to without crying. The doctor seemed to want Mom in there as well, because he spoke directly to her first.

"I need you to tell me about Stephanie's birth."

I listened as Mom told the doctor the story I heard many times. Prompted by Dr. Levine's next question about why we were there, Mom informed him of Dad's suicide and Nana's cancer. She briefly described my mood and behavior during the last two months and the struggles with the anti-depressants' side effects Dr. Adams prescribed. Hearing her recall the last three years of our lives, and my last few weeks, made me realize why I ended up in a psychiatrist's office.

Dr. Levine and I finally looked at each other. He asked me how I currently felt.

"Sad, angry, nervous, confused."

"Do you feel suicidal?"

"No, but I've thought about it and it scared me." I couldn't look at Mom; my embarrassment and shame overwhelmed me.

"Did you think about how your mom would feel if she lost you to suicide, too?"

"No," shaking my head and glancing at Mom before I started crying.

She held my hand. The doctor offered me a tissue and gave me a minute, then asked if I was taking an anti-depressant.

"No."

He looked at the names of the medications Mom had written on the form.

"I want you to try another medication. You should take it after dinner. I don't think you will experience the same side effects as with the others. Let me know. I need to see you once a week."

"I don't know if Stephanie wants me in here with her."

I didn't, because I didn't think I could ask Dr. Levine certain questions, or reveal specific details, with my mom in the room. Before I could respond, the doctor asked me if Mom could join us again next week. Then, I could start having private appointments.

I nodded.

***

Dr. Levine began the next session, every session in fact, asking me about my mood. Since I had only been taking the new prescription for a week, my mood hadn't really changed. While I felt guilty that Mom had to drive me and sit there for an hour, I felt relieved that I received the help I knew I needed. Mom did, too. We both needed time away from watching Nana as she sat in the living room all day.

Mom and I both answered Dr. Levine's questions about the topic we revisited week after week - Dad's suicide. We talked about Dad's life leading up to his death, how and where he died, and the aftermath of that day. The psychiatrist asked me if I blamed myself.

"Of course I do. I know my disability caused a lot of stress within my family. I needed more help and attention than my sister did. Mom and Dad made many sacrifices and changes in their lives because of my needs. I always felt bad that they gave so much of their time to me, particularly in high school."

My words would not be the last I spoke concerning the blame and guilt I experienced. The more I talked about it, the more I realized I could not, and should not, feel responsible for what killed my father. No one had caused it. I began to realize that Dad died of a disease – one that I was fighting. Dr. Levine said that since Dad had killed himself on company grounds, his unhappiness and stress at work most likely caused his depression and contributed to his death. No one, not Mom, not Nana, not Cris – not me – caused Dad to make that one, horrible, lasting decision.

Accepting those realizations required much more time, though.

I continued going to therapy. Although Mom didn't go into Dr. Levine's office with me, I often shared his insights or advice. We usually talked upstairs before going to bed – just the two of us. Nana didn't understand why I was seeing a psychiatrist. She didn't understand a lot as months passed. Whether it was her illness, her age, or her deliberate desire to tune everything out, Nana seemed disoriented. Her state of mind was easy to understand. Still, Mom and I experienced frustration because of it.

Summer approached after a long year. Mom decided we needed a short vacation. I slowly enjoyed activities again, and I agreed she and I could use time to ourselves. We decided to go to Disney World for a week. We had been before on family trips and, once, at Christmas with a friend of Cris' while they were in high school. This trip signified something special, though. Mom and I would be traveling alone for the first time.

Mom made arrangements for a caregiver to stay with Nana during the day. She was still well enough to get up and go to bed independently. To help her wake up in the morning, I set the alarm on the television. Neighbors volunteered to check on her. Mom and I both felt a sense of relief as we took a shuttle to the airport and she pushed me in a wheelchair to board the plane.

I was very cognizant of the fact that Mom needed as much, if not more, time off from taking care of someone else than I did. Before the trip, I told her I wanted to dress myself as much as possible. I already learned how to apply my own make-up – no mascara or eyeliner, obviously! I continued to have challenges, though, dressing myself. Still, once Mom put my bra on me, clothes became easier to maneuver with practice. Although I could eventually unfasten buttons and zippers, they never became part of my wardrobe.

Mom and I stayed near Disney World. We visited Epcot again and we walked around Disney Marketplace. In fact, we visited the Marketplace twice. It was small enough for me to walk, in between shopping and eating. I knew pushing me in a rented wheelchair wasn't exactly relaxing for Mom in Epcot, but we covered more ground and didn't have to wait on lines! Away from Disney, we toured the Forbidden City on a day it poured. The teaming rain allowed us to take the tour in a covered golf cart. The next rainy day, Mom and I saw Pocahontas, the movie that year, on Disney grounds.

We both felt blue flying home. Mom told me when we arrived home that her mood changed dramatically as we walked in the house. Many, many years later, I remembered her comment and understood exactly how she felt as I returned home from my first independent trip.

***

Life continued to revolve around taking care of Nana. Still, as I felt better emotionally and could once again concentrate on what I liked to do, I continued to work on my computer. I especially enjoyed getting online and learning how to use the Internet. From my first experiences online, I could see the potential in using the Internet to communicate more easily, and perhaps, to work from home one day. I never imagined the Internet would give me so much freedom in accomplishing tasks I never thought I would ever do independently.

To help me stay busy with my own interests, Mom gave me the idea of making my own business cards. Having a professional-looking business card allowed me to "advertise" my computer services and might lead to some work, which it did. A nonprofit organization, of which our neighbor served on the board, hired me to complete a data entry project. For a flat fee, I took as long as needed to input stacks of cards containing donors' names and addresses. Wasn't exactly stimulating, but the busyness of typing served its purpose. I finished a similar project for a local business owner. He forgot to pay me, though, and when he closed his tea room weeks later, that was that. So much for the entrepreneur in me!

**

Not being able to work or play on my computer made me realize how much I needed that distraction. One day, as Mom and I were getting ready to go out to lunch, I decided to put on a new pair of olive green loafers, just one little decision to boost my spirit that day. Coming down the carpeted stairs, my left foot turned and slipped out from under me. I landed on my bottom, and immediately, felt pain. I tried to stand up, but I couldn't put weight on my ankle. I called Mom, who couldn't help me up by herself. Nana's physical therapist was working with her and came to help. Together, they walked me to the living room.

I suffered a severely sprained ankle, which began swelling in a matter of minutes. Nana's therapist said something about RICE – rest, ice, etc. Mom brought me an ice pack. I wouldn't be going out to lunch.

For the next several weeks, in fact, I wouldn't be going anywhere. Even to my bedroom. My ankle hurt so badly that I couldn't walk upstairs. I had to borrow Nana's walker to go to the bathroom and to the kitchen. Nana's room became my room as well. I took the couch, against the half-wall of the kitchen. The pinky peach print couch became my bed.

As if my sprained ankle didn't make me more physically disabled, at least temporarily, my injury brought back feelings of depression. I couldn't sleep on the couch; my flailing body needed more room to stretch. Nana offered me her bed, but I wasn't about to take it from her. The sporadic hum of the refrigerator kept me awake much of the night. Nana's snoring didn't help me sleep, either. Yet, when I didn't hear that or the gentler sound of her rhythmic breathing, I often wondered if she had died. Those nights sleeping downstairs made me constantly think of what Mom and I discussed privately. Would Nana wake up in the morning?

My downstairs confinement easily led to a renewed sense of feeling sorry for myself. Once again, though, Mom did her best to help me - and help me help myself. She took me to the mall, pushing me in a travel wheelchair. I think she would have honored my joking request of moving my computer down if she could have carried it. When I began to doubt that my ankle would heal, she coached me to slowly walk more and more on it. As weeks passed, I hoisted myself on my bottom up and down the stairs. My healing ankle, along with my reemerging confidence, soon allowed me to climb up and down on my feet. I also gave away those olive green shoes.

***

Toward the end of 1996, Mom made the decision to look into nursing homes for Nana. The daily, mostly emotional, struggles caring for Nana drained both of us. Although she sold her condo through long-distance phone calls with Ralph, she had limited resources after we paid her debts. Mom and I never understood why her monthly retirement benefits were so limited. Close friends questioned the matter, too. Still, we thought she had enough to pay for a decent place.

I went with Mom to visit a nursing home close to us. We both liked it, but Nana could not afford it. From a list of private homes, we finally chose one after visiting it. The home seemed clean and the residents, while seemingly senile, appeared well cared for. Sitting in the nursing home, while Mom, Cris, and I answered questions about Nana, made me uncomfortable and anxious. I knew, though, that Mom had to make a decision. She and I couldn't make Nana comfortable or content any more, and Mom needed to think about her own health – for herself and for me.

Nana celebrated Christmas and New Year's Day with us. Around the fifth anniversary of my father's death, Mom and I took her to her new home. She obviously didn't want to go and her sad eyes pleaded with me to convince Mom to let her stay with us. I tried not to look directly at the older, thinner image of the woman I spent so much time with growing up. Only after we left the home did I cry with Mom.

With the staff's suggestion, Mom and I waited five days before visiting Nana. When we arrived on Thursday, the residents watched television in the living room. We recognized Nana in her pink robe and white bobby socks she never wore in her life. Her hairstyle, though, was not the shoulder-length strands that she, and later Mom, often tried to curl. Instead, these strands were gathered in a ponytail holder and sat on top of her head. Mom wanted to fix her hair. Nana seemed disoriented enough not to care. Her confusion became clearer as she talked to Mom and me

"Arlene, do you know that your father is very sick?" she asked Mom.

Mom and I looked at one another quizzically. Why was Nana talking about Daddy George? He had been deceased for seventeen years. Did Nana really lose her mind in the few days since we had taken her to that home? We just nodded and listened as she put all of her effort into speaking about her husband, her parents, and events long in the past. I think Mom sensed my nervousness because she said we needed to go home. We kissed Nana and told her we would see her in a few days.

On Saturday, Mom and I were getting dressed when someone from the home called. Nana was conscience, but would not wake up. The staff wanted to call an ambulance and have her taken to the hospital. Mom said we would meet them.

We rushed, which I can never do easily or calmly. As Mom parked the car by the emergency room of the same hospital where Nana received treatment, I told my mom to walk ahead of me. I didn't want to fall. Mom already went inside when I saw an ambulance pull up and paramedics open the back doors. Nana's feet, in those little white socks, caught my eye. I waited until the men rolled her out on the gurney. I felt silly saying "Hi, Nana" because she appeared asleep, but I wanted her to know we were with her.

Nana was admitted to the hospital, and just as we did when she stayed two years ago, Mom and I visited every day. Nana woke up, and on Monday, she seemed lively as she talked to us. I felt calmer as we left the hospital that day and the next. On Wednesday, Mom decided we needed a little distraction, so we stopped to look around a clothing store on the way to the hospital. Mom found a pair of pale blue pants and a vibrant floral blouse to match them. As we waited in line to pay, Mom suddenly looked at her watch and said, "We have to go."

The lights in Nana's room were dimmed as she lay sleeping. Mom and I sat and talked to her softly. We held her hand. She did not wake up. Dr. Ericson happened to be making rounds and walked into the room. Mom and I felt comforted in his presence. While he was talking to us, Nana's breathing suddenly became rapid and shallow. It stopped. Then, it started again. Dr. Ericson listened with his stethoscope and called it a specific type of breathing.

"It's time we call hospice. I'm going to go make the arrangements to have Adele moved to that part of the hospital. I'll be right back."

The doctor was gone a few minutes when Nana started breathing rapidly again.

"I think I better call your sister at work," Mom said. Cris was working about twenty minutes away. I went with Mom to the waiting room while she called. Cris was on her way when we returned to Nana's room.

Her breathing continued. Then, it stopped.

By the time Dr. Ericson came back into the room to inform us about hospice arrangements, Nana died.

Dr. Ericson left the room again to get a nurse, who came and said she would clean Nana. I didn't know what that meant exactly and I asked Mom when we went into the hallway. As Dr. Ericson walked in our direction, I started crying.

"I've witnessed many, many deaths. It never gets easier," he said. He then asked my mom if she thought I needed a sedative to sleep that night. I shook my head to both of them.

"Well, you have my home number if you need one." We didn't have his home number, but I didn't need it. I took a whole muscle relaxant to help me sleep that night.

Cris arrived a few minutes later. Mom either told her, or she knew from seeing my face.

"I wanted to get here before she died," she cried.

When we arrived home, I headed upstairs to Nana's room. Although she hadn't lived in it for over two years, the room reminded me of her. The yellow and white bedspread, with multicolored flowers, used to be mine. The white dresser still contained some of her clothes and other personal items. Her white wicker nightstand had a picture of the two of us in Palm Beach on it. I sat on Nana's bed when MaryLou and one of her daughters came to bring us dinner. Before I went downstairs, I heard my former teacher and friend ask Mom how I was doing.

"I've tried to prepare Stephanie for this day."

Yes, she did, and I knew, intellectually, it was coming. Still, I wondered if I could get through another loss, one just five years and eleven days after my dad's death.

A few days later, Mom and I sorted papers and found a brown envelope from hospice. It contained some information on the process of dying. The information described how an individual may reminisce about lost loved ones weeks or days before death. Mom and I wished we found it sooner.

***

Mom, Cris, Chad, and I decided that we would take a trip to Palm Beach to honor Nana's life. Five months after her January death, her ashes, in a pink floral box, came with us on a plane to Florida. We joked that we forced Nana to travel by plane, at least in spirit, after all.

We stayed in a small beachside motel on South Ocean Boulevard. Edna and Ralph, Nana's treasured friends, joined us for dinner and dog racing at The Kennel Club. None of us spent the amount of money the entire night that my grandmother would have spent on the first race. We saved some of our money to go to restaurants and shops Nana and I visited. Playing tour guide kept my mood light, at least temporarily, as I shared stories of my fun-filled summers with Nana Adele.

On the Saturday of our long weekend, we went to the cemetery and buried Nana's ashes next to Daddy George's grave. A Catholic priest from one of the local parishes Nana and I attended came to give blessings. Mom was sadly surprised that Edna and Ralph did not come; I was not. If anyone was more upset about Nana's death than we were, that person was Edna. She lost her best friend.

Our trip brought back the intense grief I felt in January. Flying home from Palm Beach signified the passing of a great part of my life. I had wonderful memories, yet it was time to move forward – again.

9
Learning to Advocate for Myself:
Dealing with the System, Fighting for Rights

Before Nana's death, while Cris and Chad lived in Austin, Mom asked Cris to research disability resources for me. At the time, I didn't follow up on any of the information she found. Now, with Nana gone and Mom working part-time in retail sales, I needed to restart my future. Doing what? I didn't know. I was not receiving the support and assistance I needed from the vocational rehabilitation, or VR, system to discover the answer.

Cris' research led me to call Advocacy, Inc., a protection and advocacy organization that works with vocational rehabilitation clients and other people with disabilities. Although I recalled seeing Advocacy's contact information on the back of a VR brochure, I didn't know about the assistance the organization provided. During my initial call, an intake specialist noted my background and briefly explained that the staff would review my case. They would then decide to accept or deny my case under the Client Assistance Program, or CAP. If my case was denied, I could appeal the decision.

About a week later, I received a call from Gwen Adair, an advocate with CAP, who informed me that my case was accepted. Gwen would act as my advocate and, although I didn't fully understand what this meant at the time, represent me to TRC. She wanted to meet and explain how I might benefit from CAP services. I assumed I would meet her in her office, but she came to our townhouse.

When Gwen and I met for the first time, we immediately developed a bond. Not only did I like her as a person, but I also appreciated her genuine interest in me, my goals, and my abilities. Gwen told me a few things I didn't want, or wasn't ready, to hear. From that initial meeting, though, she respected my decision to want to work from home. Still, Gwen wanted me to expand my world by suggesting that I step out into the community independently.

As apprehensive as I felt to attempt this new independence, I knew Gwen's suggestions could bring me out of my own existence. To begin gaining greater independence, Gwen told me about the Houston Center for Independent Living (HCIL). Run by and for individuals with disabilities, HCIL offered self-advocacy training, peer support services, and computer classes. Gwen and I called HCIL before she left our first meeting. She told one of the directors a little about me, and then I spoke for myself. I expressed my interest in attending computer classes. When Tony mentioned what the computer instructor could teach me, I told him I already knew how to do most of those tasks. I agreed to attend a class once a week. Mom drove me.

HCIL exposed me to something I rarely saw - people with disabilities working. Most used wheelchairs, had their own offices, and did real work. I had never seen so many individuals with various types of impairments in a workplace. Seeing this surprised me – maybe I had already read too much about employment barriers faced by the disabled. HCIL's computer instructor, who also had CP and earned a college degree, seemed interested in sharing his expertise with me.

My mom dropped me off for a few hours per week at HCIL. I promised Gwen that I would think about using the paratransit system, MetroLift, to travel to and from the center and other places independently. This experience frightened me on many levels, however. I never boarded a mini bus or a cab alone. What would happen if, rather when, I fell? What if the driver did not understand my speech? One of my more frightening worries made me wonder how I would defend myself if someone tried to hurt me.

The time it took to apply MetroLift services did not alleviate my fears. Still, as Dr. Levine explained during my now monthly session, I needed to demystify something I feared to learn the actualities of it. Gwen encouraged me to take small steps, too, to increase my independence and self-confidence. Leaving the house alone meant I needed to be able to lock and unlock the back door, but I didn't have the ability to use a key. I thought this inability would stop me from attempting new adventures. No such luck! Gwen addressed the issue with my counselor, and soon a keyless system was installed on our sliding glass door. With a simple touch of a button on a remote that looked like a garage door opener, I finally unlocked the door myself after it locked automatically. When I was approved to take MetroLift, Gwen even offered to follow the bus or cab while I took my first trip. I didn't take her up on the offer, yet I appreciated her understanding and support as I took these steps.

***

As Gwen became more familiar with my case files at TRC, she and I met with my VR counselor, a deaf man. David and his sign language interpreter once visited my home because I couldn't come to his office. Although the interpreter understood me and conveyed exactly what I said to David, I wondered why the two of us were paired in a counselor-client relationship. Didn't each of us have enough challenges communicating with people with typical hearing and speech? How could David really observe my physical difficulties and needs when he constantly watched his interpreter? Wasn't I supposed to look at the counselor directly while speaking to him? If his interpreter didn't understand me, however, shouldn't I look at her?

Gwen's presence and assistance made me more comfortable with these communication challenges. She and I both explained my employment goal of finding a telecommuting position using my computer. When David questioned my desire to work from home, I explained that, although I applied for paratransit services, home employment would save me time and energy. Getting ready for a job in a workplace required personal assistance. Mom, my sole caregiver, worked about thirty hours per week. David then mentioned my eligibility for home health care services. I blatantly informed him I didn't want that assistance.

"Wait a minute, Stephanie," Gwen said. "David is trying to increase your independence. Having home health care does not mean that you must work outside the home. It would, however, help you and help your mom. Why don't we look into it?"

"Okay." I did like the idea of relieving Mom of some of the work it took to care for me.

***

In a matter of weeks, my life changed dramatically. I took MetroLift to HCIL once a week. At first, a young woman with CP scheduled my rides. Despite giving her my travel days and times, however, I had rides coming when I did not need them. So, I scheduled my own rides over the phone. I learned how to be better understood by people used to deciphering impaired speech, yet couldn't understand my first or last name. Arranging my rides offered lessons in patience for me – and for the person on the other end of the line.

Patience and the paratransit system, in fact, go hand in hand. My mom and I heard horror stories of people waiting for hours to get to and from places – Nana drove me back and forth from Project Independence for this reason. If I wanted to go anywhere by myself, however, I had to take MetroLift. . . and become used to waiting, calling, waiting, calling, and many, many other frustrations in using paratransit. These problems clearly and realistically supported my desire to find home-based employment.

Life at home changed as well. I was approved for eleven hours per week of home health care. Mom worked a somewhat regular schedule in retail, so she and I decided that I should have a caregiver come in the late afternoon on the two days she worked into the evening. She liked the idea of me not being alone all of the time she worked, and we both appreciated having someone to help me bathe, do household chores, and prepare a meal that would not end up on the kitchen floor.

Having a stranger assist with my intimate needs required new ways of thinking. I never explained to anyone how to bathe me, wash and dry my hair, or help me dress. Step by step, I thought about the exact ways in which my mom assisted me for over twenty years. Fortunately, my very first caregiver, Pat, worked with children with severe disabilities during the school day. This was also her first experience with home health care. We seemed to learn how to work together – together! Pat's experience with individuals with much more severe impairments than mine, and her surprise in what I did independently, made me more comfortable.

With each of these new steps, Gwen and I kept in constant contact with each other by email. She encouraged, but never pushed me, to think about specific plans for my future. When I became apprehensive or anxious about trying something new, she provided more details about it, then backed away to allow me to make my own decision. I frequently had the feeling that Gwen thought I should pursue college, or try to obtain employment outside my home. I knew, however, that she respected my decisions and choices. At our next meeting in the vocational rehabilitation office, Gwen's advocacy for my goals and interests became even clearer.

Gwen and I walked into the next meeting to request a vocational evaluation. At the table sat David and his interpreter. Before we began the meeting, a woman walked in the room and closed the door. I didn't know who she was. I looked at Gwen.

"Hello, Ann. Why don't you introduce yourself to Stephanie?"

"Stephanie, I'm Amy Mann. I'm the manager of this office."

I nodded. I felt nervous, but I always felt nervous at meetings, especially those discussing my uncertain future. Gwen sensed my anxiety, because she started by summarizing what we discussed at the last meeting – my goal of working from home. As always, Gwen asked me plenty of questions so she did not put words in my mouth, and I spoke as I became more comfortable.

"Stephanie, you receive disability benefits, don't you?" the office manager asked.

"Yes," I answered, wondering what the question had to do with our discussion.

"Well, I don't think you should bother trying to get a job. You should just stay home and collect your benefits."

I sat there in shock. I didn't know whether to cry or scream; even if my shock allowed me to do either, I knew I couldn't let my emotions show. I looked at Gwen, who I seemed just as angry or angrier.

"Ms. Mann, working is about a lot more than earning money. It's about having something to do, using my skills and abilities, and feeling good about myself."

I only had one more message to add to Gwen's.

"I want to have a purpose in life."

I don't remember what Gwen said to end the meeting, but I followed her lead as we quickly left the room. We went to the waiting room, where the first words out of Gwen's mouth included:

"I'm glad your mom wasn't in that meeting!"

"Definitely," I nodded and laughed. My nerves went into overdrive, though, and I started to worry if I would ever receive vocational rehabilitation support.

"Let's go outside to talk as we wait for your ride."

I felt like we left the enemy camp as the accessible doors swung open into the warm air. I didn't mind the heat as I finally felt like I could breathe again.

"Okay, we need to get your case out of this office. When I get back to my office, I'm going to write a letter to the regional manager to transfer your case. I know some good counselors who will work with you. Don't worry, let me do my job. We will not let you fall through the cracks.

Stephanie, don't forget, this is your life. You have a right to say what happens in it."

***

Four weeks later, I took MetroLift to an office much farther from home to meet my new VR counselor. Gwen gave the regional manager specific names of counselors to choose from to provide me with services. My new counselor, Beth, had severe arthritis in her hands, Gwen mentioned. Although I was very skeptical of her willingness to help, she seemed empathetic to my situation and interested in me as an individual, not just in my disability. Beth took the time to learn that I was becoming an aunt for the first time. She congratulated me when I emailed her that my first niece, Natalie Noelle, was born in 1999.

Beth agreed with Gwen in scheduling a vocational assessment to better narrow my employment goal. As with every service I received, Gwen stressed the fact that I had choices in providers for this assessment. With a list of providers in hand, I researched the Internet to understand what this assessment would provide, and what question to ask in choosing a provider. Gwen came over one day, and together, we called providers to ask questions. Writing down the responses we received, my advocate encouraged me to make my own choice. I chose the provider who gave the most thorough answers. The owner of the company told me about the employment specialist who worked for her, too.

Over a period of three days, I took a regular cab, paid for by TRC, to an office building to take various tests and to demonstrate my physical abilities, or lack of. When I walked into the office, the evaluator and I recognized each other and figured out we knew each other from, of all places, a department store restaurant which he previously managed. Robert saw me with Mom and Nana many times, and this sense of familiarity made me more comfortable. In between assisting me with mostly academic testing, Robert noticed me doing things he said he didn't think I could do.

As I unwrapped my lunch on the first day, he came over and asked if he could help me.

"It's okay. I need to do this myself. My mom and I talked about this last night. She reminded me that I need to show you how independent I can be."

"I see that, but what if I want to spoil you?"

"I do like being spoiled," I said, smiling.

Robert wrote that comment in his report, which listed my high scores on the tests I took. He also included a description of the typing I did on the last day of the assessment, when I somehow brought my keyboard with the keyguard with me. The report emphasized my painfully slow typing speed and my need for another home computer. Unlike any other report I read, however, it highlighted my abilities and my potential.

***

Gwen thought I needed one more evaluation before I chose an employment provider to search for jobs with me. To address my typing speed, she asked Beth to provide an assistive technology evaluation. The evaluation was done by a man with cerebral palsy from Texas Rehabilitation Commission who came from Austin to observe me using the computer at HCIL. Although I continued going to the center, I no longer attended computer class. I didn't feel I learned much, and the instructor's attempts to teach me programming went nowhere. Instead, I spent my time volunteering by doing office work, mostly filing. I was glad that the assistive technology evaluation occupied my time that day.

Mom dropped me off to ensure that I arrived on time. As I got out of the car, I noticed a man in his accessible van parked next to us. I didn't think about it until

I saw him driving his motorized wheelchair into the classroom soon after I walked in and sat down at the computer with my keyboard. He introduced himself as Jim, and asked me to spend a few minutes typing as he observed. After a brief time, he said we could go meet Gwen in the conference room.

Jim mentioned some new technologies on the market, including some type of dot attached to a user's forehead to control the mouse cursor. He didn't think that I had enough head control, however, to use it. My speech was too impaired to use speech recognition software. Just as I became discouraged, he mentioned something he wanted me to take home and try.

"This is word prediction software. It will help you type a little faster and reduce fatigue."

Jim went on to explain that, as I typed, the program would present a list of words based on the few first letters I hit. When I saw the word I intended to type, I would strike the number on the list and the rest of the word would appear, saving me time and keystrokes. This new process, of course, required practice. The software program's benefits to a one-thumbed typist soon became obvious. That is, if I could practice with the software.

I took the disk home and loaded the software onto my computer, which was becoming obsolete. The program didn't seem to work because of my slow computer. I emailed Gwen and explained the problem. She and I discussed what needed to happen next.

"I think we need to ask TRC for a new computer. You will certainly need it to reach your employment goal. In the meantime, you need to choose an employment provider."

"I have."

***

I received a new personal computer around the time I began working with Bonnie, the employment specialist where I received my vocational assessment. Since she had the report from the assessment in the office and worked with Robert, I assumed she had a clear picture of my abilities and goals. I should have known by then – assuming anything was wrong.

"I have an idea. I know you and your mom enjoy shopping. Why don't we get you a job as a mystery shopper? Your mom could take you to stores and you could get paid to critique the service and your shopping experience."

"Um, no. That's not what I want to do. First of all, my mom works in retail and isn't home every day to drive me everywhere. That job wouldn't promote any independence or use many of my abilities. I just received a new computer and I want to use it to accomplish independent work."

I think Bonnie had good intentions, and maybe she wanted to secure a job quickly. Working with her, though, gave me the feeling that she had not assisted many intelligent individuals with physical disabilities. I had enough experience, though, to know finding the type of job I wanted would not happen easily or quickly.

***

My time and connections at HCIL benefited me weeks later. A staffer from the center called and told me about a south Houston lumber company looking for a home-based worker to manage a database. I listened to the job description, and then I excitedly called Bonnie.

Within days, Bonnie drove me forty-five minutes from home to interview in a log cabin-like building. The few women in the office were dressed in jeans and long-sleeved casual blouses, so my professional clothing, and not just my involuntary movements, stood out. Bonnie and

I sat down as a couple of men started talking and asking me questions. One man, younger than the others, seemed impressed with my answers and what I confirmed I could do. I tried to control my nerves as much as possible. Bonnie and I left with a good feeling.

That night, I gave all of the details to my mom, who seemed tickled that her daughter might help sell lumber for a building products company. Mom spread the news to Cris. On the phone, I heard her telling my sister about the cute guy who conducted the interview.

"His name sounds very European."

I picked up the phone. "Warren von something . . . I'm not sure how to pronounce his last name."

Cris finished it for me.

"Yes, that's it!"

"We went to high school together. If you see him again, tell him I said 'hi.'"

***

"Hi, Warren. Come in."

After I was hired, Warren made the trek out to my home to deliver the disk containing the existing database. He gave me some information about my responsibilities and explained how I might be able to expand their potential customer base in the future. Essentially, I would build their contacts and send them faxes through the computer to advertise the company's products. At the time, the job sounded challenging and I wanted to prove to everyone, including myself, that I could work from home.

As Warren was leaving, I mentioned my sister and showed him a picture of her.

"Oh, yes. I remember her. What a small world!"

For the first time, my case with TRC closed successfully. Gwen and I kept in close contact, even as she transferred to Austin a few months later. She continued to help me from afar. Her teaching me to become my own best advocate led me into the future when she was no longer there.

***

Once I learned the essential job responsibility of building and organizing the database, along with regularly sending faxes, Warren encouraged me to use the Internet to search for more potential contacts. I enjoyed developing research and writing skills, and felt proud when my supervisor asked how I added the company's website link to email. My part-time job ended up teaching me what I could teach myself.

Although Warren and I primarily communicated over email, his leaving the company to continue his education altered my job. I soon met my new supervisor as he kindly delivered materials I needed to my house. To my surprise, he invited me to a company barbeque one night. A friend from HCIL, Phillip, drove and went with me. I didn't know anyone, but I appreciated being included and recognized for the small roll I played in the company.

During my second year of working at home, my job became busywork. I easily tied up our one home phone line for hours by sending hundreds of faxes per week. Aside from trying to schedule these during non-business hours (and when Mom didn't need the phone!), I became bored and unchallenged. I wasn't ready to give up my job, but I realized I wanted more. I needed more.

Soon, one phone call led me on my next path.

10
College:
Studying, Working

One afternoon in the spring of 2000, Mom came home from her new position as a part-time Kindergarten teaching assistant and asked me a question.

"Steph, did you know there's a new Houston Community College on the beltway?"

"No. Where?"

"It's right passed I-10, off the beltway. Ten minutes from here. It looks like a new campus."

That information planted a seed in my head to start growing.

***

The next day, I looked up the campus online. I saw that the campus had a counselor for students with disabilities, but I couldn't find a direct phone number or email address. So, I called the main number. What did I have to lose, except for a little dignity?

I prepared myself for the person on the phone to hang up on me. She didn't. I asked to speak to the counselor who handled disability accommodations.

"Oh, that's Dr. Russell. I'll transfer you to her office."

A minute later, I was speaking to her.

"Hi, my name is Stephanie Torreno. I'm interested in taking some courses. Can you understand me? I have cerebral palsy."

"Yes, I can understand you, and I can tell that you have CP! Stephanie, have you ever taken any college courses?"

"Actually, I have some credits from years ago when I took computer classes at the central campus. I was in a program called Project Independence. I earned about thirty credits."

"Well, you should be in our system. Why don't you give me your Social Security number? I'll look you up and call you back."

I was glad she asked for numbers instead of asking me to spell my name. People who haven't heard my speech in person seem to have an easier time understanding numbers rather than letters. She took my phone number, too.

Dr. Russell called me the next day. I sensed the excitement in her voice.

"I have a copy of your grades right here. They're terrific! I would like you to come see me so we can talk about what's next for you."

We set an appointment, and she gave examples of disability documentation I needed to bring. I told her my mom would come with me.

***

Mom and I walked the short distance to the first office in the building. The door wasn't heavy and had a lever handle, making it easy to open. We sat in the small waiting area, and through the window to another small office, I saw a woman with short, reddish-brown hair. Sitting at a desk, she looked at me through thick glasses as I looked at her.

We walked into Dr. Russell's office. I introduced myself and my mom. As always, I felt nervous and didn't quite know what to say. The counselor took a magnifying glass from a coffee cup holding pens and studied the papers in front of her. Mom and I glanced at each other, guessing she had some type of visual impairment. In the many years I would come to know her, I easily forgot about Dr. Russell's disability.

"It's obvious you can do college-level work. Do you know what you would like to study?"

"I've been told that I'm a good writer. I've read some information about technical writing. Maybe I should work on a certificate in that area."

"Well, nothing must be decided right now. I'm going to give you a schedule to offer you some ideas. Do you think you will start in the fall?"

"Yes. I work at home right now, but I need more of a challenge." Mom prompted me to tell her a little more about myself and how I used assistive technology to work on the computer. And, of course, my mom embarrassed me by telling Dr. Russell that I graduated cum laude from high school.

At the end of the meeting, Dr. Russell told me that I needed to take a placement exam. Since I had been out of school for a while, my scores would tell her if I needed to take any developmental classes.

"You'll need accommodations for the test. Why don't we meet again in a few weeks and arrange your testing."

***

Dr. Russell wrote my accommodations for the placement test. I received double time to complete the exam, the use of a scribe, and the use of a computer to type my response to the essay question. My testing took place in the testing center with other students.

I completed the reading portion of the test independently, selecting my answers to multiple-choice questions on the computer with my keyboard attached to it. In the math section, though, I needed a scribe to write calculations for me. A testing assistant looked like she didn't know how to help, but she sat with me and tried. After trying to write a few problems, she went to speak to the testing director.

"I can't understand her."

"Where is her mother?" the director asked, loud enough for me and other students to hear.

"Excuse me, my mother isn't applying to take classes here. I am. If you cannot understand me, than you need to find someone who can. My mom shouldn't have to help me."

After a few minutes, Dr. Russell came in and sat next to me. She used her bold ink pen to write the calculations I asked her to jot down. When I figured out the answer, I chose it on the monitor.

For the essay question, Dr. Russell moved me to a small office within the larger room. My keyboard came with me. I settled down and started typing some notes to form my response to the question about the pros and cons of extracurricular activities in school. My typing was

110

slower than usual, though, as the accessibility features I needed weren't set and I didn't have my word prediction software. I tried to open the Control Panel in Windows to try to set StickyKeys, but I couldn't use the mouse. Panic overcame me, and when I looked at the monitor again, what little I typed had disappeared.

Looking out the window to the larger room, I got the attention of the director. I tried not to cry as I told her I needed Dr. Russell again. Someone called her office. I only imagined and didn't want to know what they said about me.

The counselor came in a second time after walking from her office. I tried to control my emotions as I explained what happened and why I couldn't use the computer as I typically did. I asked Dr. Russell if I should forget about the whole test.

"Most certainly not! We're going to forget about the computer. I'm going to write for you. Now, let's make some notes about what you want to say. You need to tell me how to capitalize and punctuate, too."

For almost an hour, Dr. Russell sat and wrote for me. When she didn't understand my speech, she asked me to repeat what I said. She asked me questions before writing something to clarify any details.

I finally finished the test. Waiting for the results, I began questioning my decision to go back to school.

**

I called Dr. Russell's office to schedule our next meeting. Her secretary didn't understand my speech over the phone, so I emailed Dr. Russell, who was on vacation. I continued to question my decision to go to college, thinking about the many arrangements I needed to make involving transportation, caregiving, and completing the coursework itself. I tried to keep remembering Gwen's advice about directing my own life and believing these many issues would work out to allow me to continue my education.

At our next meeting, my attempts to believe I could coordinate everything won over my doubts.

"I mentioned last time that I wanted to work on another certificate, but I've changed my mind. I think I want to start earning an associate's degree."

Dr. Russell smiled and laughed out loud in agreement. "I wanted you to reach that decision yourself. Your test scores indicate that you are prepared for college-level reading and writing. In math, however, your score fell just below the minimum to take College Algebra. You will need to take one developmental class."

I was disappointed in my math scores, but I knew I had forgotten so much. Yet, I wondered if the testing situation had affected my score. Most of all, I wondered how I would complete my work in class and at home. Before these concerns lead us to the discussion about specific academic accommodations, the counselor expressed concern about my mobility, particularly in crowded hallways.

"Oh, I'll use a walker. It will help me transport my books, too."

She liked the idea, as did Mom. Next, Dr. Russell asked me about transportation.

"I'll use MetroLift."

"I use the system to get here, too." She shared some tips about scheduling subscription service, since I would have regular trips to and from campus three days per week.

Dr. Russell then explained my rights and responsibilities as a college student with a disability. Although Mom joined us in each meeting so far, I needed to act as my own advocate. The counselor couldn't discuss my grades, or anything related to school, without my permission. I looked at Mom and laughed, "I'll tell you what I want to tell you!"

To receive my accommodations, Dr. Russell explained that, before each semester, I needed to make an appointment with her. She would write, date, and sign letters to my instructors, listing the academic accommodations I needed to "level the playing field" and to complete the same requirements of any other student. Discussing these accommodations one by one, the counselor included the need for a peer note taker, the use of a scribe or computer (with assistive technology) and extended (double) time for in-class assignments and exams and tests, and, with her suggestion, the need for a regular, larger table and chair in class. Instead of going to the testing center, I would test in the small computer lab next to her office. She reassured me that my accommodations could be modified if needed. On the first day of class, Dr. Russell instructed me to give a letter to each instructor to establish a rapport with them.

This opportunity will also introduce them to my impaired speech, I thought.

During my first semester, I took Government I and Intermediate Algebra. Dr. Russell approved that balance of classes, and she approved each instructor!

***

With the beginning of classes just weeks away, I had many preparations to finalize. Since I hadn't used a walker in years, I needed a prescription from my doctor to buy one partially covered by insurance. I picked a black and blue tripod with a pouch hanging down the middle of it, where I stored my lunch. My book bag hung with one strap on each handle, weighing down the walker. I reminded Mom of that as she made me practice walking and my clumsy movements occasionally tipped a wheel off the ground.

I called MetroLift next to schedule subscription service, giving the days and times I needed to go to campus. My first class met at 11:00, so I said I needed to arrive at 10:00 as recommended. I knew I would spend many more hours at school than needed, but I didn't want to arrive late and cause myself more anxiety. My disability already set me apart in class. I didn't need to point it out by walking (and rolling) in after other students.

One of the final preparations became the most challenging. My caregiving schedule needed to change for someone to help me get ready in the morning. Mom left for her school much earlier than I needed to be ready. I already changed my services to another, or two or three, home health care agencies by this point. Having a caregiver come on time, help me dress, prepare my breakfast (if Mom didn't leave it for me), make my lunch, and leave when I was picked up seemed like a workable arrangement. What we eventually learned!

On the Saturday before classes began, Dr. Russell invited me to take a tour of the building. With my walker, I followed her secretary down the first main hallway. She pointed to the faculty restroom, with one door that locked with a pushbutton, that Dr. Russell already cleared permission for me to use. Mom walked along the tour as well, reminding me to stand up straight and to try to keep the walker's wheels on the floor. The secretary also repeated Mom's reminders. I knew I needed my books and other necessities to add weight to my three-wheeled aid to move more smoothly and confidently.

I just need to start classes without people watching me, particularly Mom.

***

I arrived at school an hour early on the first day. The first obstacle I encountered involved opening the door to the building; I couldn't open it while pushing my walker. I later advocated to change that. With an hour to kill, I went to the library, entering it when someone opened the door for me. I looked around, glanced at some periodicals, and tried to relax before my first class. At 10:45, I made my way down the first hallway and used the faculty restroom. My classroom was right next door. In the crowded hallway, I happened to see Dr. Russell, who I surmised was checking on me. Months later, she informed me of a brief conversation between her and my instructor.

"She has cerebral palsy, so I'm guessing her difficulties are primarily physical. Is that all I need to know?" my first college instructor asked.

"Yes, that's all."

Sitting at the only table beside the rows of desks, I put my folder and book on top of my rectangular piece of Dycem to prevent them from sliding. The instructor came in and introduced himself to the class. Mr. Foster called roll (not my name, though), passed out the syllabus, and reviewed the course requirements. With reading assignments, quizzes, tests, and a paper summarizing a current book due in twelve weeks, I realized why I was only taking two courses!

Mr. Foster came over at the end of class to write my name on the roll sheet. He saw the envelope I had on the table, and I should have given it to him first as it had my name on it. Instead, he patiently listened as I spoke and spelled my last name. I then gave him my letter. The instructor asked if I had any questions and reassured me that I could talk to him whenever necessary.

With an hour between classes, I walked to the student lounge to eat my lunch. Crowds always heightened my anxiety, and this mob of older teenagers was no different. I had difficulties navigating my walker around the tables and chairs already occupied. Somehow, I found an empty spot and ate, but the commotion of the pack of students made me want to leave fast. In the subsequent weeks, I stayed in the classroom once I realized it was empty the following period. Less stress and less moving.

My first day continued with a longer walk to Intermediate Algebra. The laid-back instructor's requirements didn't seem too demanding and I knew I would not need to devote hours of study to the course. I found myself, in fact, helping my note taker and other struggling students who had taken the course multiple times. Weeks into the course, I mentioned my classmates' difficulties to Dr. Russell, who encouraged me to ask them to come see her. I don't know if they ever did, as students' disability disclosure and accommodations remained confidential. As Dr. Russell herself scribed some of my course exams, I wondered if others followed up on receiving the supports they seemed to need.

I continued to work at home a few hours per week. My job, however, was busywork, and with little contact with anyone at the company, I wanted to quit. Mom reminded me that I paid whatever financial aid didn't cover and I needed what little pay I earned, but school was my priority now. A few weeks into second semester, I made up my mind and wrote my letter of resignation.

***

Second semester at HCC began with a bumpy start. I took the second half of government, and while I wanted it with Mr. Foster again, my female instructor became a favorite, too. During the first class of College Algebra, the instructor noticed my staring at the pre-test. Coming over to me, she asked if I needed a pencil. I couldn't fault her for making assumptions, but I really wanted to ask her what she thought I would do with one.

"No, I am unable to write my work." I thought I should give her my letter of accommodations at that point, instead of waiting until the end of class. Unexpectedly, she opened the letter in front of me and seemed to want to immediately discuss the supports I required. Whether my look of embarrassment influenced her or not, she folded and held the letter.

"Just look at the problems and think about how to solve them. I'm not grading the test."

For the next half hour, that is all I did.

After I told my mom what occurred in class, she encouraged me to do what I thought I should do.

The second day of classes, I went into the office and asked to speak to Dr. Russell. I tried to quickly tell her about the incident. Although I didn't want to sound as if I was complaining, I explained how uncomfortable I felt in the class.

"I'm sorry you felt that way. The truth is that instructor expressed her discomfort in having you in class. I think you should change classes."

My schedule changed for both classes. Since I typically arrived an hour earlier, I took an earlier Government II course from the same instructor, had a break, and then took College Algebra with a more accommodating instructor. I ended up turning in the few assigned homework problems in my own very large, but decipherable, handwriting on many days.

Going to class earlier during the day turned out to accommodate my new opportunity.

***

The day after I quit my home-based job, I could hardly wait to get home from school to share my news with Mom. The minute she walked in the door, I began talking.

"Hi, Mom. It's a good thing I'm not working at home anymore. I have a new job!"

"What? Where?"

"At school. Dr. Russell hired me as a work-study student!"

If I wasn't taking an exam in her office, I always found a reason to see Dr. Russell on the three days a week I had class. Careful not to occupy her time as she served hundreds of students, I saw her as I went in and out of the small computer lab within her office. If her office door wasn't closed, I said "hi," or went in for a few minutes. On the day I shared my news of quitting my monotonous, dwindling job, I never expected her reply.

"Good. I've been waiting for you! I want you to work for me. I want to show other students what you can do."

My work-study job revolved around my courses, as Dr. Russell knew that school remained my priority. I worked after class for a few hours, typing her schedule in her electronic appointment calendar. My duties grew to include other tasks, as I wanted to prove to others, and myself, what I could accomplish in the office. Without a full-time secretary now, the busy counselor depended on much assistance from regular, part-time student workers and work-study students to run her office with the high standards she set.

I adjusted my MetroLift subscription to accommodate more hours on campus. My frequently long waits for rides continued, as they did for other riders, including my counselor turned supervisor. I found myself running back and forth to call the dispatchers from Dr. Russell's office, though, I had a new reason to belong there. The office served as my workplace.

***

"So, now that I'm a paid employee here, may I advocate for an automatic door to this building?" I asked Dr. Russell one day. I grew very tired of having to wait for someone to aid in my entering the building, and hurt my arms in attempts to enter myself.

"Why did you wait until now? Go ahead! You know which person to contact, don't you?"

My letter to the president of the Northwest College included an explanation of my contact with Advocacy, Inc., which handled complaints regarding architectural barriers.

118

Although an investigation informed me that the building's doors met the weight standards of the Americans with Disabilities Act, they still posed a barrier to me and other students. I felt that students in wheelchairs or those with walkers, or anyone with challenges, had the right to enter and exit the building independently.

A few weeks later, two pushbuttons were installed inside and outside the building to open one of its eight doors. One of my fellow students, who used a wheelchair due to CP, thanked me for my advocacy in promoting the installation. I joked with him that my name should appear on a plaque under the pushbuttons! As I reached and pushed the button one day for an approaching instructor using a wheelchair, his sincere thanks rewarded me. Finally, I returned a favor with a simple gesture.

***

Second semester ended on another high note with an awards dinner, during which I received one of Dr. Russell's Golden Star Awards. Mr. Foster walked with me to the elevated stage to accept the heavy, embossed paperweight. As she always did, Dr. Russell attended to every minute detail, bringing a gift bag for me to carry my award off stage.

With credits from Project Independence and the nine I earned that academic year, I was now a college sophomore. In addition, I became an aunt for the second time, as Madeline Adele Farrell arrived in April, one day before her big sister turned two. Three days later, I celebrated my twenty-eighth birthday – on the 28th.

***

While college continued to prove challenging and rewarding, receiving help from caregivers on school mornings equated to pure frustration and anxiety. A caregiver did not want to come for only an hour or two, or if one came, she was late. Her tardiness, more than a few minutes, made me lunge into frantic frenziness. On the hopeful assumption that my ride might come on time, I couldn't take it if I wasn't ready. I never missed a ride, though, because my neighbor, a retired school nurse, came over more than once to button a blouse or make a lunch. Sometimes, I arrived on campus emotionally exhausted.

Changing home health care agencies didn't help. Once, for example, a supervisor from another agency appeared at my back door as I was getting ready for school. My caseworker hadn't given her my phone number! When I explained my schedule, she said she didn't think she could find anyone to help me.

"I know what you're trying to do. Good luck."

Know what I was trying to do? Yes, I was trying to live an independent life and earn a degree.

At least she was honest. I moved on to another agency, with a different plan.

"Mom, I don't think I can depend on caregivers on school days anymore. I'm too frustrated. I'm going to have to get up earlier and do what I can do myself. Will you help me with whatever you can before you leave?"

"Yes. I'll get up fifteen minutes earlier and put your bra and top on and then I'll do your hair."

During my remaining years in college, Mom and I made this arrangement work. With more practice, I became better, and quicker, at dressing myself. I even began putting on my own panty hose and tights, though I only wore those on occasionally cold mornings. I still received home health care, but a caregiver came on days I usually didn't go to school. Usually on Tuesdays and Thursdays, a caregiver came in the morning and stayed longer to help me with tasks I didn't have time to do every day. My caregiver made lunch for the day and prepared one for the next. With the afternoon to myself, I worked on my assignments.

"Summer is for relaxing," Dr. Russell responded as I shared my idea of taking one summer course.

"No, I want to take one class online. I'm going to be working here anyway! Why can't I register for just one course? I'll work on it between helping you, and at home, too. I don't want to take ten years to earn my degree."

I don't know who was harder to persuade, Dr. Russell or Mom. I won the battle, however, and took my first online class, Art Appreciation. As Dr. Russell joked later, this class might not have been the best one to take online! The instructor required a student-produced drawing, which I did over and over until I was somewhat satisfied. In the office, I continued doing the computer work Dr. Russell needed me to do. I also began tutoring students in both math and English. As promised, I took a week off and Mom and I took a road trip to Fredricksburg, Texas.

***

Perhaps I became a little too confident in my abilities to handle college and work when I convinced Dr. Russell to register me for nine hours in Fall 2001. History, English, and Finite Math seemed manageable, with English only meeting two days a week. I became more confident in my work, too, although Dr. Russell encouraged me to trust my instincts more without asking for her approval. With two new part-time student workers that year, my job continued to offer great satisfaction – and fun!

Armenia and Boyan shared the responsibilities of office receptionist, with Armenia working in the morning and Boyan working in the afternoon. Dr. Russell held a meeting with the three of us before classes began to clearly outline her expectations. Since I worked for her more than a few months, she used me as an example of how to dress appropriately, how to speak to both parents and students, and, most importantly, how to respect individual differences. Respecting individual differences took on a whole new meaning for me as Dr. Russell led by example each and every day.

I enjoyed getting to know my two new coworkers. Armenia educated me about her native Brazil during our downtime, and I enjoyed sharing insights into our crazy American culture. Boyan and I shared a love of music on Friday afternoons. Most of all, my new friends demonstrated great compassion toward me and others with disabilities pursuing higher education.

Dr. Russell's guidance in selecting great instructors led me to one of my most favorite college professors. Dr. Botson taught me U.S. History for two semesters. History became enjoyable and challenging as Dr. B., as he is known, gave stimulating lectures and led thought-provoking discussions. In addition, his willingness to accommodate my physical limitations went beyond the guidelines listed on my letter of accommodations. His exams, for instance, included multiple-choice questions and two 250-word essays. After I took the first exam in one two-hour period, he asked if completing it all in the same day was too tiring. When I admitted it was, he allowed me to type one essay one day and the other on the next day. Since we had a choice among essay questions to answer, he simply drew a line in some so I couldn't read all of them. Dr. B. certainly didn't offer preferential treatment, but his own accommodation preserved some of my energy needed for the rest of the day.

My emotional energy was spent one Monday after walking into the office. I had been assigned an essay in English that was due Wednesday. I had the next day to write it, but I already knew I wasn't going to finish it. As I rushed into the lab to hide my emotions, Dr. Russell saw my face and followed me. She closed the door. Before starting to cry, I told her my predicament.

"I didn't want to do this."

"What? Take nine hours?"

"No, cry. I know I have tomorrow at home to work on it, but my typing is still so slow. I also have other homework. But I know I can't ask for an extension. It's homework!"

"Why not? You can ask. Your instructor should know that your rough draft is pretty close to your final draft. Ask him if you may have a few more days."

A few moments later, my instructor came in the office to tell me something I missed when he sent me to the lab to start my essay. I quickly regained my composure.

"Mr. Clark, I know the rough draft is due Wednesday, but I think I may need a few extra days. Is that okay?"

"Sure. One of your classmates already asked for more time as well. Turn it in next Monday!"

I was embarrassed to have become emotional over something so simple. My academic achievements meant so much to me, however, and I always wanted to turn in my best work. That assignment was a definition essay in which I chose to define and explain what 'advocate' meant. As part of the assignment, I emailed Gwen in Austin and included quotes from her response in my paper. I received an 'A.'

***

I learned my lesson and returned to taking six hours the next semester. Dr. B. warned me how hard he was going to work us, and I wanted to enjoy his class and my first psychology course. As I began to think about choosing a major when I transferred to a four-year university, I already thought about pursuing my interest in psychology. Although I hadn't taken one course in the subject yet, the psychology I read fascinated me.

Coming into work one day, I asked about one of the students who also worked on campus. Though I didn't know her name, my description of her let Dr. Russell and Armenia figure out whom I meant.

"Well, as I waited for my ride the other day, she came up to me and asked what was wrong with me. I told her that I have cerebral palsy, but she didn't understand me. She thought I kept saying something about cereal!"

Dr. Russell joined in my laughter. Then, she became serious. "There's nothing wrong with you! You have a physical disability, but it's not something that's 'wrong.'"

"I don't think I ever thought of it in that way!"

"Well, you should. Do you know what I want you to do with your disability?"

"What?"

"I want you to go above it, below it, over it, through it. Do not allow your disability to stop you from doing anything you want to do. Ever."

I received lessons such as this one all of the time from Dr. Russell. Then, I went to class!

**

On a routine morning when my ride was really late, a regular cab (paid for by MetroLift) showed up. The driver, instead of pulling into the carport, got out of the car in the guest parking area. I needed him to get my walker from the patio. When he didn't understand me, I simply pointed. As he went to gate after gate until I nodded that he had found the correct one, I noticed his gait was a little shaky. His unkempt appearance worried me.

He finally began driving me to school. His driving seemed erratic, and I was greatly relieved when he pulled up to the college. After he opened the car door, his hands touched my bare legs and stayed there. When his hands started to move up and down my legs, I began shaking and forcefully hoisted my body out of the cab. I grabbed my walker he already took out and walked to the building.

Allowing someone to open a door for me, I quickly made it to the office. Armenia saw the panicked look on my face and called Dr. Russell, who came and listened as I told her what happened, and thankfully, what didn't happen.

After I calmed down, Dr. Russell walked me to class. I wanted to go, even if my thoughts were elsewhere. I think Dr. Botson was shocked when I walked in late. He joked, "I thought I was in the wrong room when I didn't see you," but I knew he sensed something was wrong. I quietly made it through class and went back to the office in a hurry. Dr. Russell asked me into her office again and told me she had called the police.

We filed a report and I skipped my next class. I remained in the office the rest of the school day. Dr. Russell called Mom, who came and picked me up after work. I received many hugs that day from the two women I love dearly.

A police sergeant called the next day and led me to believe that the driver had a criminal record. Even if I wanted to, I don't think I could have pressed charges. I have heard other stories, far worse than mine, from women in wheelchairs during my numerous trips. I realized I was lucky, but vulnerability and fear never left after the incident.

***

Just as I did the previous summer, I made up my mind to take another online course and work under twenty hours a week between June and August. With a second counselor in the office, students with various types of disabilities kept us busy. The other counselor relieved Dr. Russell from having back-to-back appointments with students throughout the day. Working with another counselor in a small space required some adjustments, however.

An advocate from Advocacy, Inc. came with a student for an appointment one day. I think I had met Karen through Gwen once. Also, Karen's name came up when Gwen recommended other rehabilitation counselors to work with me. When Gwen transferred to Austin, I heard that Karen became an advocate with CAP. Karen and I spoke for a few minutes, and I mentioned that I hadn't been in touch with Gwen in a while.

Before I left for the day, Dr. Russell called me into her office. She asked me to close the door.

"What did I do now?" I joked. My beloved 'boss lady's' face didn't reveal her usual jovial self.

"Nothing. You always assume you've done something wrong," Dr. Russell remarked. Her tone was serious when she asked, "Stephie, did you know that Gwen was sick?"

"Well, I hadn't heard from her in a while. I wondered if anything was wrong."

"Steph, Gwen had lung cancer. She died a few months ago."

Tears started welling in my eyes. Dr. Russell knew what Gwen's influence, and friendship, meant to me. I told Dr. Russell several times that I wished I had returned to college sooner, but she reminded me that I did it when I felt ready. Gwen's advocacy on my behalf had begun to prepare me to feel ready.

My sadness continued the next day at work, though I was glad knowing Gwen knew I returned to college. Still, when I asked the other counselor a question about Gwen's death since she knew her as well, her response startled me.

"Why are you thinking about that? You shouldn't be thinking about it."

I grieved for my friend. My thoughts and feelings were not wrong, but I kept them to myself the rest of the day.

When the wonderful 'boss lady' was not in the office, it changed into a different atmosphere. With Dr. Russell on vacation, I concentrated on my job, on my class, and on what Gwen taught me about advocating for myself.

I continue to display a framed picture of Gwen on my bookshelf.

***

Armenia and Boyan finished their respective degree plans and transferred to universities, leaving me with two new coworkers and a work-study student to get to know and help. While my two former officemates looked forward to attending larger schools, I began wondering where I would continue my education. I wanted to take every class I could take at HCC, and of course, I wanted to work for Dr. Russell as long as possible. I knew, however, that I would begin attending a university in a year.

I began discussing possibilities with Mom. Dr. Russell shared her desire for me to go to the University of Houston. She thought I should live on campus and become more independent.

"Dr. Russell, I like living with my mom. I'm not just opposed to living on campus. The classes at UH are way too big and I don't feel comfortable in large environments. I know I can't manage all of that walking. I don't want to use a wheelchair if it's unnecessary."

I knew she wanted the best for me, and we continued this discussion. By then, Dr. Russell heard my story about visiting Houston Baptist University with my parents before I graduated from high school. I explained how I felt the campus was an ideal environment for me, physically and academically.

During the fall semester, Dr. Russell announced she was going to a luncheon. She smiled at me as she said, "I'm going to check out this HBU place."

"That's not part of your job!"

127

"Yes, it is!"

When I returned from class that afternoon, I found a white coffee mug with the blue and orange HBU Husky on it. I carefully carried it and peeked into Dr. Russell's office.

"Thank you for the cup."

"You're welcome. I like the school. I think you can go there!"

I only had to figure out how to pay for it. And settle a couple of other concerns as well.

***

During my last academic year at HCC, Dr. Russell again asked me to participate in a seminar at the annual faculty symposium. I joined a panel the previous year, speaking about my experiences as a college student with a disability. Not everyone understood my speech, though, and my anxiety took over the experience. I hesitantly agreed to speak again. This year, the symposium was held at a Marriott hotel on a Saturday. Mom dropped me off, and I met Dr. Russell in the lobby.

After we took the elevator to the correct floor, I began seeing some of my instructors in the hallway, including Dr. Botson. Seeing people I knew, along with walking around before entering the conference room, eased some of my nervousness. Dr. Russell, another work-study student, and I took seats behind the table in the front of the room.

Introducing her two work-study students, Dr. Russell spoke briefly about the ADA and the basic procedures for disability accommodations. She then allowed me to speak. From my seat, I described my journey back to school, my beginning at the community college, and the accommodations that helped me function in and out of the classroom. I acknowledged my instructors who worked with me in achieving my academic success. Then, my coworker rose to the podium and spoke about his experiences with a learning disability.

We answered questions toward the end of the conference. I mentioned something about realizing I was far from the 'normal' college student. An art instructor who I had gotten to know from working at school responded.

"Stephanie, there is no such person as a 'normal' college student."

Great point!

One instructor asked me about my future plans. I expressed my hope to transfer to HBU. A couple of audience members started suggesting different universities, some out of state. I explained my preferences in choosing this school. These back and forth exchanges went on for a few minutes. Finally, a familiar voice ended the conversation.

"She's going to HBU," Dr. Botson exclaimed!

Dr. Russell told me at school the following week that many individuals from the previous conference made comments about my improved speech. Almost all of what I said was understood.

***

In April 2003, I celebrated my thirtieth birthday at school. One of my coworkers, who took Literature and Film with me, told me our instructor said we should be twenty minutes late. Not suspecting a thing, I walked into the classroom to a large "Happy Birthday" sign and balloons everywhere. Our instructor, whom I had had for English II, obviously supported this surprise. The party continued after class in the office, where Mom met me!

Over cake and ice cream, I visited with several of my instructors whom I had known over those past three years. I shared my plans with them. Although I had two more courses to squeeze in that summer, I knew I would graduate in August. Mom and I visited HBU recently and met with an admissions counselor, who thought I would receive a substantial scholarship. We made an appointment with the professor who handled academic accommodations, but had not met with him yet.

I thought I had a good grasp on everything I needed to handle before I transferred to HBU. Just like with my balance, however, unexpected obstacles can make me lose my grasp.

***

The last summer I worked at HCC, I registered for two classes I needed at HBU, Community Health and Speech. I would take the health online, and attend a five week speech class. I was acquainted with the speech instructor, and while I didn't really want to take the class because of my ever-present anxiety, I thought I would earn the required credits before transferring.

I attended the first class and found the instructor humorous, and perhaps a little irreverent. He reviewed the course requirements and assigned a brief introductory speech to be delivered the next day. After a few questions about the assignment from other students, and funny comments from our instructor, I raised my hand.

He looked at me. "And you're the pain in the ass student everyone knows!"

I laughed, but I didn't consider his comment at all funny. I never asked my question, and I found myself in a hurry to leave when class ended. Frequently, when I try to rush, I fall. That's exactly what happened as I stood up from my chair. I fell flat on my stomach. Before I knew what happened, the instructor helped me to my feet. Thanking him, I did my best to grab my walker with both hands and carefully walk out of the room. I went to the restroom to collect myself before returning to the office.

Dr. Russell saw me walk in the door. I tried to hide my shock and embarrassment when I told her what occurred. She really liked this particular instructor, but admitted he could be somewhat over the top. We left it at that.

After thinking about the incident that night, and calming myself - and Mom – down, I went into work the next morning and dropped the class. I honestly told Dr. Russell I signed up for one too many courses; the rocky start convinced me that I needed to drop that one. So, instead of going to class, I remained in the office, working and taking my course online.

I can't say I was surprised when the speech instructor came into the office after my absence on the second day. Out of the corner of my eye, I saw him head toward Dr. Russell's office. A few minutes later, he came into the lab and asked if he could speak to me. I nodded and moved to the table in the center of the room.

"I understand you dropped my class. I apologize if my comment offended you. It was a joke."

"I was offended, and I thought it was inappropriate."

"Will you come back to class?"

"No, I've decided I've taken on too much this summer. I'm taking another course, I'm working here, and I'm preparing to transfer to HBU."

"Are you sure you won't reconsider?"

"No. Thank you for your apology, though."

***

My three years ended with another surprise – the President's Award. Dr. Hodges, the President of Northwest College, presented me with this honor for "outstanding achievement in academics, college leadership, and community service." This surprise added to my mix of emotions in receiving my Associate of Arts degree, leaving the workplace where I enjoyed helping and learning from others, and most of all, already missing my beloved "boss lady," counselor, and friend.

11
University:
Earning a Degree, Teaching
a Few Lessons

The same day Mom and I met with an admissions counselor at HBU, we scheduled an appointment with the professor who held the title of 'disability coordinator.' I mentioned to the secretary that I would bring my disability documentation and a copy of an accommodations letter from HCC.

"Oh, Dr. Williams will see that you need accommodations."

While that statement was obviously true, her words stunned me. If anyone who worked for Dr. Russell made that comment to a student, he or she would hear a mini-lecture regarding procedures, individual differences, and most of all, presumptions! Dr. Russell, however, didn't serve students here. I felt that my college education was beginning again in learning, and teaching, about individual differences.

***

A week later, Mom and I returned to the campus building with the large dome, the Hinton building. We took the elevator to the third floor and entered the glass doors to many of the professors' offices. The same secretary led us to Dr. Williams' office. I didn't expect the man to be so old.

We sat down, and I did most of the initial talking. I gave the professor a copy of a report from TRC that documented my disability and a copy of my accommodations letter from HCC. In addition, I prepared a summary outlining the assistive technology I use on the computer. I didn't want any remaining questions unanswered regarding my physical abilities. He asked a few, though, and seemed to want to address them to my mom rather than to me. We both redirected his attention.

"You have a note taker in class?"

"Yes, a classmate shares a copy of his or her notes with me. We usually go to an office and make copies after class."

"We couldn't ask a student to do that."

"Why not? The arrangement works very well."

He looked at the papers again to avoid answering. Dr. Williams then brought up the issue of using a computer to take tests and complete in-class assignments.

"I don't know how we would let you use a computer to take tests."

"You mean this campus doesn't have a room or a lab with a computer for me to use."

"Of course we do. I just don't know how we could accommodate your needs. I don't think this is the school for you. I think you need to look into state universities."

All I could do was look at my mom, who had tears forming in her eyes. I was too nervous and upset to speak. I let Mom talk because I thought she might explode.

"You're telling us that you can't help Stephanie achieve her dream. She has wanted to attend this university ever since she graduated from high school. Her father's death put that dream on hold. Stephanie has worked very hard at HCC and is graduating with a 3.9 GPA. She's already been accepted here. You're not going to help her."

I don't remember what else was said as we left the meeting. In the car, Mom and I started crying. I felt angry. As Gwen taught me, anger means the time has come to start advocating. I didn't want to attend another university; I wanted to earn my bachelor's degree at HBU. I needed to advocate to make that happen.

***

Between my final spring and summer semesters at HCC, I continued to believe I would attend HBU that fall and double major (as required) in English and Psychology. I visited campus again independently, taking my incomplete transcript with me. The science department had a question regarding the biology course I took; I took a course description from HCC's catalog to show it to the department. I also visited campus for another reason – to meet the Dean of Academic Affairs.

I don't recall how the meeting with Dr. Looser was scheduled. I think I emailed him to explain what occurred with Dr. Williams. However it came about, I found myself sitting in a large, beautifully decorated office holding the same papers I took to the previous meeting. This time, though, the man I met listened carefully as I spoke, asked questions, and expressed interest in my success and potential. When I suggested a call to Dr. Russell to further explain my accommodations, Dr. Looser took her phone number. Standing up and starting to navigate my walker out of his office, I explained I needed to go to the science building.

"You're going to walk all the way over there? It's awfully hot."

"I know, but I need to show this course description. I can handle it."

"I'm sure you can, but it's such a long walk for a quick matter. Please have a seat again. I'll call someone to come to you."

I smiled at the assistance I was now receiving. My advocacy was just beginning, but I made a start. Dr. Looser began to clear obstacles in my path. Many more arose.

***

"Dr. Russell, I gave your number to Dr. Looser at HBU. He'll probably call you soon to talk to you about me," I told her the next day.

"Thanks for letting me know. You're a little late, though! Dr. Looser called yesterday. I think you found an advocate on campus."

If my academic accommodations were in the process of being arranged, my financial matters were a different story. I already registered for two fall courses, and seeing the tuition statement sent me into full-blown panic. At HCC, I paid the remainder of what financial aid didn't cover. I couldn't begin to pay even a small percentage of my new tuition. I wasn't going to be working, either.

Money matters became worse when I received my financial aid letter in the mail and Mom called me at work about it. She told me I was going to receive a little over a hundred dollars per quarter. That might have covered one textbook! I immediately started fretting, and of course, Dr.

Russell wondered why. Neither of us understood why I was going to receive so little in aid.

My ineligibility to receive a scholarship also upset me. I could only physically take six hours per ten-week quarter. This schedule was considered part-time, and part-time students couldn't receive scholarships. I thought this exclusion was unfair, particularly because I wasn't choosing to attend part-time. My physical limitations made this choice for me. So, before I went ahead with an idea, I spoke to Karen Stanfill at Advocacy, Inc. She agreed that I should write a letter to the President of HBU. In my letter, I recalled how my parents and I met Dr. Hodo twelve years earlier, and why I delayed my college education. I stated how hard I worked academically in the last three years at HCC, and why I felt I deserved a partial scholarship. I can't believe I had the nerve to write this letter! Again, what did I have to lose?

***

I already decided to have my vocational rehabilitation case reopened with TRC, which was now the Department of Assistive and Rehabilitative Services (DARS). I guess the agency finally figured out that some individuals cannot be "rehabilitated" if they never had certain abilities from birth! DARS needed to know what I had been doing the last few years, and how I needed their help. I expected a battle with them; I wasn't disappointed.

To receive financial assistance from DARS, I knew I had to continue pursuing other sources of financial aid and scholarship. The counselor agreed to help me, with one condition - I needed to attend school full time. My attempts to explain how my physical limitations drained my energy and added additional time to most activities went unheard. I required assistance in having my voice heard.

Karen accompanied me to my next meeting. I was quite surprised when the counselor informed me that she contacted the university and asked if I could be driven around campus in a golf cart (as security officers used). She argued that this arrangement would conserve my energy, thus allowing me to take a full course load. Never mind that relying on others to transport me on campus limited my independence.

"What about the other activities taking nine hours entails? The reading and studying for each course? Is someone going to assist me with typing papers?"

Karen acknowledged her surprise when she asked, "You type all of your papers yourself?"

"Yes. Typing is part of my writing process. I have to give myself more time."

Karen looked at the counselor, who did not say anything. Before she could respond, Karen asked her, "Will you please show us the policy stating that a college student is required to attend full time to receive funding?"

The counselor left the office to look for the documentation Karen requested. We sat a while before Karen told me, "She can't find it because it doesn't exist. We'll ask DARS to pay the rest of your tuition for fall. Keep working on other sources, too. You and I will meet here again after your first quarter."

"Okay. I'll pay for my books."

"What? You don't need to do that."

"I want to. I saved money for them."

***

The phone rang on a Sunday evening. Mom answered the phone and called me from downstairs, "Steph, it's for you. Someone from HBU."

Who would call me on a Sunday from school? I suddenly became anxious as I hit the button on my speakerphone.

"Hello, Stephanie. I'm Sharon Saunders, the Vice President of Public Affairs at HBU. Dr. Hodo received your letter and asked me to call you. I'm going out of town this week, but I wanted you to know that you will be receiving a scholarship. You'll be getting a letter in the mail with the details. Next time you are on campus, let's meet and talk."

I was on my way.

***

The fall quarter finally arrived. I began my MetroLift subscription on the Friday before classes began. I wanted to pretend that it was my first day and locate classrooms, restrooms, and lounges, and buy my books. Without Dr. Russell's guidance, I needed to familiarize myself with the campus before navigating through the crowd. Putting my textbooks in my book bag weighed down my walker, preventing it, and me, from flying into the air.

On the way from the bookstore to the Hinton building, I tripped on the sidewalk and plopped down. Oh great! I did not tell Mom about this fall. I got myself up, and discovering my scraped knees, continued walking to the building. I pushed the button to open one of the doors and carefully walked around the first floor. Finding a restroom, I struggled to push the door open, leaving my walker outside. I cleaned off my bloody knees and composed myself. My first fall on campus was actually a relief. Why not get it over with before school started? I would go more slowly in the future, and learned where cracks in the sidewalk could trip me.

Sitting by the elevators before taking one upstairs, I saw a petite woman, not much taller than I, reach for the elevator button before turning my way. She smiled and asked, "Are you Stephanie?"

"Yes."

"I'm Dr. Maddox."

I immediately smiled and enjoyed meeting my Abnormal Psychology professor. She sat next to me on the bench and asked what I was doing on campus that day. I told her I wanted to get a feel of the grounds before the first day rush. We talked for a few more minutes.

"I heard what happened with Dr. Williams. I just want you to know I'll work with you in any way I can. I look forward to seeing you in class Monday."

After I took the elevator to the second floor and located my psychology classroom, I went down to the first floor again and out the building to find my second classroom. I walked the short distance to a smaller, two-story building. Neither of its doors was accessible to me. A coach passing by held the door. My classroom was the very first one. Still, with only ten minutes between classes, walking quickly from one building to the next, with a possible restroom break, would be challenging.

Luckily, all of my classes during my years at HBU met in one of three buildings clustered together. So, DARS' idea of having security ride me around in a golf cart wouldn't have conserved much of my energy. The student center, with the bookstore and an easily accessible restroom, was a little farther, but certainly within a manageable distance. As my stamina increased, though, my tolerance for not being able to enter buildings independently did not.

***

I scheduled MetroLift to take me to campus extra early; the drive was a little farther from home and I needed plenty of time once I arrived. All of my time on campus allowed me to feel part of the college community. Once classes began, I always found something to do to pass the time, though I saved most of my reading and writing until I came home.

Since I met Dr. Maddox that previous Friday, I felt somewhat relaxed in her class the first day. I grew more comfortable as I saw several students older than I was. After our professor reviewed the course overview and requirements, she asked each one of us to respond to "Where would you rather be today?" Most students replied with answers of fun places, and of course, some said they rather be sleeping!

I said, "I don't want to be anywhere else. I waited a long time to get here."

Dr. Maddox smiled and nodded, telling everyone of our meeting by the elevator.

Walking to the next building with minutes to spare, I followed girls into the restroom, letting them hold the door for me. I was in too much of a rush to try to lock the stall door, so I only closed it. The next thing I knew, a young woman pushed open the door and immediately apologized. I quickly finished and left the restroom.

Finding the classroom I located on Friday, I sat in the first row. Two people could sit behind the table; I didn't worry about needing more room. Then, the young woman from the restroom encounter came in class and sat next to me. We both apologized to each other and laughed about it. Kelly, who had a familial connection to disability, became a great friend to me on campus.

An older man, obviously the professor, walked into the room and began the Old Testament course with a prayer. After the usual first class practicalities, he came over to me and spoke to me.

"Even if I didn't just call your name on the roll, I knew you were Stephanie. I've been receiving all kinds of email about you from Dr. Looser. I also know about cerebral palsy because I have a nephew with CP."

I could only imagine what Dr. Looser had written in all of those emails! I was grateful to him, though, for informing my professors of my accommodations. Still, I took it upon myself to give my professors my own accommodations letter. If they had any concerns, I referred them to Dr. Looser. I think it was understood that I would not go to Dr. Williams' office again, and I never did.

My first quarter at HBU made me feel as if I were two students. In my psychology course, I aced exams and received an 'A' on my research paper (which, I told Dr. Maddox, I was required to write after she had expressed concerns of too much work!). The Christianity course, however, tested my academic abilities. I studied in the same manner in which I always studied, and had thorough note takers. The professor thoroughly confused me when he encouraged me to skip reading and only find the answers to test questions. After all I had done to secure a scholarship, I barely passed the exams. Perhaps I should have stayed in the classroom on exam day, instead of going to the noisy computer lab, while the professor led a prayer before the test! He assisted me in advocating for a smaller, quieter computer lab in which I took my tests.

By the time I registered for winter quarter, I completed the request for Dr. Maddox to become my academic advisor. I never met my advisor when I first registered, and I felt having one of my professors as my advisor would benefit me as a student. My request was approved, and Dr. Maddox advised me many times, both academically and otherwise.

When I received my second tuition statement, I took it home and studied it before sending a copy of it to DARS. I did not understand why my tuition was considerably lower than last time. Then, I noticed a credit card payment listed with my financial aid and scholarship. I certainly didn't use the credit card I shared with Mom. I couldn't have afforded the payment!

During the next school day, I returned to the financial aid department, bringing the credit to the attention of one of the counselors. She didn't believe me at first.

"No, this line isn't my payment. Whatever financial aid and scholarship didn't cover, DARS did. It's not my credit, but I wish it was!"

Another student's payment had been credited to my account. The counselors who finally figured that out were grateful for the mistake I caught. I laughed out loud when they asked me if I was a math major. Of course, I never knew whose payment that was, but I hoped he or she was grateful.

I was grateful, too. After receiving so little in financial aid during the first quarter, I sat down with a counselor. She reviewed my income and my expenses, including the amount I contributed to the household, my prescription medications, and my personal needs. Upon this review, I was awarded more in aid. As the quarters rolled along, though, the less I needed. The harder I studied, the more scholarship I received. Part of receiving a scholarship included writing a letter to the donors, which I gladly did. My academic difficulties in Old Testament only threw me off temporarily.

My first quarter ended with a washout – literally. I arranged with Dr. Maddox to take my final exam two days early to avoid having exams back to back. While Houston was forecasted to have torrential rain that day, the rain hadn't started until I arrived on campus. Dr. Maddox saw me walking to take my exam and was surprised I had shown up on such an inclement day. I told her my mom was picking me up.

The rain had been pouring very heavily for a while by the time Mom arrived. She came in the building and met Dr. Maddox, who had come to get my exam. Dr. Maddox offered to help us out to the parking lot, which had one to two inches of water. We put my walker, book bag, and us into the car. Mom pulled out of the parking lot, and, seeing my professor in front of us, we headed home.

Mom drove on Fondren Road under Southwest Freeway, less than a mile from school, when we noticed the rising water. Seeing a Wendy's restaurant on the right, Mom wanted to pull into the driveway. It was too late; the car stalled and water started seeping inside. When we opened the doors, the water rushed in, making it difficult to get out. Although I managed to exit the car, walking through the high water proved enormously challenging. I felt like I was going to fall when, all of a sudden, a man flung me over his shoulder and carried me into Wendy's. Both drenched, Mom and I hung out in the restaurant for hours. People around us, watching the weather and the pile-up of stalled cars, offered us dry clothes they had in their cars and assistance in getting our things out of Mom's car.

Mom and I never made it home that night. After waiting for the totaled car to be towed, the driver dropped us at a hotel off the freeway. We stayed the night, took advantage of a breakfast buffet, and then rented a car to drive home.

I studied for my Old Testament final exam with rain-soaked notes and a textbook with pages that stuck together. Two days later, I took my exam. I'm sure I didn't do well. Earning an 'A' in Abnormal Psychology and a 'C' in Old Testament, I completed my first quarter at HBU.

***

By second quarter, my complaints of the lack of accessible doors were finally heard. The Director of Campus Services installed a push-button door in the student center, where I often ate lunch, went to the bookstore, frequently visited the coffee bar. Though he mentioned having an accessible door installed in the restroom in the student center, I could manage that door, and I wouldn't walk all that distance just to use the restroom. Accessible doors were also installed in the two smaller buildings I entered each day. Never mind that in one building, my professors had to come downstairs if I needed to talk to them because the '70's construction didn't include elevators.

One day, I watched a bored classmate sitting by the entrance to the student center, pushing the button repeatedly to open the door. After the third time, I finally had it!

"Do you know why that button was installed? I had to request it so that I, and other students, could come in and out independently. Do you think you should play with it?"

"No."

"Then don't!"

I really wanted to ask him if he would be around to let me in and out if the door stopped working. I figured I had made my point, though, and gave the goof something to think about!

Another time, Dr. Wilson, a sociology professor who became memorable to me for a number of wonderful reasons, pushed an overhead cart into the building. As I passed by, he said, "This door really comes in handy, doesn't it?"

"Yes, it does."

I wondered if he knew I requested its installation. Before I even took one of his classes (which I almost didn't), this particular Dr. D. Wilson, one of three on campus, always encouraged me or shared a joke when seeing me roam around with my walker.

***

Course credits weren't the only ones I had to earn at HBU. The university required all students to earn Spiritual Life Points to further their religious education. If students failed to earn SLPs, they didn't graduate. As an incoming junior, I needed to accumulate just over thirty SLPs, compared to the ninety required of freshman. I wanted to start attending events and groups as soon as possible to receive points, and to feel more involved in the college community.

My initial attempts to earn SLPs created more stress than spirituality. Convocation, always held on Thursday morning, was a great event to receive points and experience fellowship. Since my classes met on Mondays, Wednesdays, and Fridays, though, I had to travel on a non-class day to participate at Convo. If students didn't arrive on time and have their IDs swiped, no points would be earned. No matter how early I scheduled a MetroLift trip, the system's chronic unreliability took my anxiety to a different level. I tried to attend Convo on the first Thursday of the month to receive two points, and my caregiver met me there for lunch afterward. After several close calls of delayed trips and running, or walking fast, across campus, I looked for other opportunities on class days to accumulate points. With volunteer activities I couldn't do, and mission trips I couldn't take, finding these opportunities presented somewhat of a challenge.

***

Dealing with the paratransit system continued to be frustrating and tiring. Waiting for rides on campus wasted lots of time. I read as I sat on a bench inside the main entrance to the university. Most of the time, however, I watched the cars pass by and hoped to see a cab coming my way. After fifteen minute intervals, I went into the nearby registrar's office and called MetroLift. I tried to make my call quick, but nothing related to the system was quick.

One afternoon, I asked a secretary I knew if I could use a phone. She kindly agreed; however, the registrar came in and spoke to me.

"There's a pay phone outside. I think you need to use it. You shouldn't come in here anymore."

I looked around at the many faces in the office, including, ironically, Dr. Maddox. My anger and frustration

146

were about to explode. I tried to calmly explain to her what everyone in the office would no doubt overhear.

"I am unable to use a pay phone because of my limited dexterity. I cannot put the coins in the phone and would have great difficulties dialing the phone number." Never mind spending a fortune in quarters.

After making my call, I quickly left the office. When my ride finally arrived, I hid my tears on the way home.

During the next school day, someone from campus police came into my speech class and handed me a message. I would now wait for my ride in the security office, where I could use a phone any time I needed one. Of course, MetroLift had challenges finding me on the opposite side of campus, even after several months. I made many friends with the security team as they saw how long I waited each day to go home. The officers, and especially Tina, the dispatcher, assisted me immensely.

Funny, the registrar always had a kind word to say to me after that incident.

***

The second quarter flew by quickly, with Christmas break a few weeks after it started. Although I hoped to take Speech much, much later at HBU, the course was a prerequisite for my other courses. Before I began the course, I met and talked to the professor because I didn't want any surprises. He shared descriptions of one individual presentation and one group presentation, both toward the end of the class. Along with Speech, I took New Testament with a different professor. Both classes went well.

Before I knew it, spring quarter arrived. As a psychology major, I needed to take Introduction to Statistics. This math course scared me, along with the fact that it was taught by the Dean of the College of Education and Behavioral Sciences. I knew Dr. Brown from talking to him around campus, so I shouldn't have been intimidated. Of course, I was.

Walking into class ten minutes late (guess why!) on the first day didn't help my nervousness. Dr. Brown stopped introducing the requirements and greeted me. By this quarter, I knew several of my classmates, who offered to take notes for me. At the end of class, Dr. Brown came over to me and knelt down to talk to me at eye level. I explained my lateness, and he laughed and said I didn't miss anything. He looked at my accommodations letter and then mentioned some ideas he had for me to do my course work.

"Let's meet in the lab where you take tests. I want to show you some software you can use to help with your calculations."

Standing up to grab ahold of my walker, I knew everything would work out in his class as he guided my uncoordinated right hand to the handle.

My other course served as one of two psychology electives. Human Growth and Development didn't necessarily interest me, but I wanted to take a class from Dr. Maddox again. My classmate Kelly also enriched the experience.

After Dr. Maddox lectured about birth and the newborn stage, I raised my hand and asked if she wanted me to share what happened to me at birth. I hadn't expected to do this. With the lecture and discussion about typical development, however, I thought everyone in the room could guess that my birth was atypical. For a few minutes, I spoke about Mom's difficult delivery, my coming into the world blue and not breathing, and my subsequent diagnosis. Dr. Maddox thanked me after class and again at the beginning of the next class. I quickly mentioned that I had forgotten to say that Mom had been induced. My professor seemed to feel that this detail mattered considerably.

***

Finally, I read in the quarterly bulletin that an SLP group was meeting on Wednesday afternoons. Staying on campus a little later worked for me, and I could easily participate in the group, which involved reading and discussing *The Purpose-Driven Life*. The group's leader, Chuck, was one of the counselors on campus. When I came to the first meeting, I was the only student there. Chuck and I waited for others to come. Finally, he gave me a copy of the book and asked me to begin reading it. We would meet the following week and see if anyone else joined us. I assumed Chuck would cancel the group if no one did.

Chuck again saw only me the following week. I had read the first few chapters and we started discussing the material. I guessed we would form a group of two. Although we attempted to discuss the book, we often ended up talking about other subjects. I became grateful to have my private SLP group.

I needed that time during the quarter when Dr. Maddox entered the classroom with tears in her eyes. One of her students in another class committed suicide. She talked about him for a few minutes, expressing the shock, sadness, guilt, and every other emotion I knew all too well. Suicide certainly came up in the few psychology courses I had taken, as I expected. This lesson differed. While I didn't know the student, that someone on campus had taken his own life reminded me that Dad's death and its aftermath were never far away. After class, I noticed a few students comfort our professor as they related their own stories involving suicide. I was one of them.

As soon as Chuck met me that afternoon, I knew what we would talk about that hour. His face expressed the same emotions as Dr. Maddox's did. When I shared my experience with my dad's suicide, we had an intense discussion about the issues surrounding it and the questions that remained. We both seemed to need that hour.

One of the following weeks, I located Chuck on campus and told him I felt completely overwhelmed. The end of the quarter neared, and I felt tired. He told me he was having one of those days as well. I told him my mom agreed to pick me up when I called her, so we didn't meet that afternoon. In the weeks we met, I earned many SLPs, and more importantly, gained a friend and counselor when I seemed to especially need one.

***

During the spring of 2004, Mom decided to put our townhouse on the market. With Nana gone, we didn't need a third bedroom. Mom had been cleaning out closets and making minor improvements. She wanted to see if the house would sell and, if it didn't, she would take it off the market by the fall.

Mom received an offer the following week. We were shocked! When the potential buyers requested that we move within weeks, we panicked. We not only needed to find a two bedroom townhome, we both were extremely busy at the end of the school year. Mom negotiated with the buyers to allow us to stay until the beginning of May.

Around Mom's birthday, May 8th, we moved across the street to a similar townhome complex. The townhouse needed lots of work to brighten our new home. The work couldn't begin immediately, though. Three days after moving, I took my final exams. I enjoyed complaining that those were the worst few days to move! I did well on my exams, ending the quarter with two 'A's.' With Mom working a few more weeks, I spent my school break supervising the removal of layers of wallpaper from the dark green kitchen - and unpacking.

***

I registered for one class, a writing course, during the summer. My professor, Dr. Michalos, and I became acquainted with each other on campus. I knew she was a challenging professor, and I prepared myself for five weeks of intense writing assignments. What I enjoyed most of all, though, besides learning how to write more effectively, was getting to know Dr. Michalos. She took a deep interest in my abilities, and expressed concern about the lack of accessibility in certain places on campus.

During one class, Dr. Michalos recalled the time she broke her leg on campus. Since her office was upstairs in Atwood I, the building without an elevator, her office had to be moved to the first floor. She humorously described sharing a tiny office with another professor. Worse, and perhaps most embarrassing, was the restroom situation. Each time Dr. Michalos needed to use the restroom, it had to be cleared because her wheelchair had to prop open the door since it wouldn't fit through it. When my professor mentioned that Chuck, my SLP group leader, injured his ankle that summer and used crutches to get around campus, she said the two of them thought of me.

"I only had to deal with such obstacles temporarily. So does Chuck. We know you have to navigate this campus every day."

One of the last assignments in the course involved interviewing a professional who regularly wrote in the workplace. I chose to interview Karen at Advocacy, Inc. Although I could not interview Karen in person, I emailed her questions and then typed a final copy of her responses. As part of the assignment, we presented a summary of our interviews to the class. I suddenly realized why that speech course was a prerequisite - most classes required oral presentations. Before giving them, I always felt highly anxious, which I learned was natural. No matter what, though, I talked my way through each one!

Shortly after that assignment, Karen contacted me. She surprised me with news that she nominated me for an award from the Texas Rehabilitation Association, of which she was a member. I had won! The ceremony, in which I received the Promethean Award, took place a week later in San Antonio. With short notice, and my class still in session, I didn't think Mom and I would attend. We had family to visit there, though, which convinced us to go. Splurging on plane tickets, Mom and I made a quick, fun, and really memorable trip to receive my award, which I dedicated to Gwen.

I told Dr. Michalos the reason I would miss class on Thursday, the last day of the summer school week. When she asked if I was coming back to class, I giggled and confirmed I would return on Monday. I didn't know she would share the news with the college community! When I returned to campus a few days later, people whom I didn't even know were congratulating me.

***

My new status at school continued through the fall, when my picture and news of my award made the campus newspaper. The public relations office took my story one step further and wrote an article about me for the campus magazine. One of the office staffers interviewed me and took my picture with Dr. Brown, who contributed a nice quote about having me in class. Before publishing it, the writer gave me a copy of the article to proofread at home. I returned to her office with a correction.

"Actually, I received the award from the Texas Rehabilitation Association, not Texas Rehabilitation Commission." I didn't explain all of my difficulties with TRC over the years. By pointing to the error, I also hoped she realized that the line wasn't a complete sentence.

She edited the line in the article to form a sentence, although she said the mistake in the organization's name wouldn't have mattered. It certainly mattered to me.

The attention and persistence I dedicated to writing papers and essays convinced me to change my second major from English to Writing. Unaware of HBU's Writing major, I learned about it from Dr. Michalos. The university was one of few that offered the major at the time, with degrees in Creative Writing, Professional Writing, and Technical Writing. I didn't want to major in Creative Writing, but I didn't know which of the other two to choose. On the advice of a writing professor who happened to be downstairs, I choose Technical Writing! He thought it was more marketable.

Beginning my second fall quarter, in 2004, I registered to take a sociology course with Dr. Wilson and another writing class. Although I heard Dr. Wilson's course involved intensive writing, I didn't know how much until I attended class on the first day. With a short paper due each week, I worried about how I would complete the amount of writing. Speaking to Dr. Wilson after class, I appreciated his honesty and understanding as he encouraged me to take another class, since I would be writing constantly in my other course, too.

For the same credit, I ended up taking Business Ethics. The amount of writing was manageable. In fact, for my writing class, I rewrote two papers from other courses. These courses included oral presentations, too. Business Ethics became one of my favorite courses, and I never would have taken it without my professor-who-wasn't-my-professor's advice!

***

I found myself in an unexpected comfortable situation on the first day of the winter quarter. In Brain and Behavior, I presented Dr. Johnson with my letter of accommodations. While no professor questioned the information or required me to visit the current disability coordinator, Dr. Johnson was the first. Before he told me of his requirement, though, he read my bulleted points indicating my academic needs and asked a question.

153

"What should I tell other students when you are not in here on exam days?"

With some baffling questions from educators over the years, this question was new. I didn't know how to answer, let alone why he asked it.

"That matter really isn't other students' concern." Many of my classmates knew me, and they knew I needed computer access to take tests. If they didn't know that, couldn't they figure it out? We were college seniors, after all.

I reluctantly made an appointment with the female professor who now handled accommodations. Although she didn't have much to say during our brief appointment, her aloofness made me uncomfortable. Why did she want to know if I had an advocate? Wasn't I advocating for myself?

Dr. Johnson's class challenged me. With all of the disorders we discussed in class (including CP), he didn't seem to understand mine. I considered myself lucky that I passed his exams when other students took his course multiple times. Toward the end of the course, he assisted me in the extra credit assignment by lending me a booklet. That I received an 'A' on my research paper, and a 'B' in the course, impressed both of us!

Along with another writing course, I completed my writing internship on campus. While Dr. Michalos asked me if I wanted to intern at Advocacy, Inc., I knew I would have difficulties with transportation. So, I tutored other students in writing and editing papers. In between weekly sessions, I worked on my assignments when I didn't have other students to help.

***

My spring and summer credits officially made me a senior. I kept a copy of my majors' requirements on my desk and began crossing out classes as I completed them. One credit I didn't earn was a biology lab credit. Although

I completed the course at HCC, I didn't take the lab (actually, I checked with HBU to see if my geology lab counted and I was given misinformation). Dr. Maddox didn't see the point of me watching a lab partner do the work. Dr. Looser agreed and waived the requirement.

In summer school, I took two courses for the first time. Desktop Publishing challenged my physical skills in keeping pace while trying to use the trackball and MouseKeys to format text and graphics. The professor worked with me on keyboard alternatives to accomplish the same tasks. Since he cancelled at least one class each week, I used the additional time to work in an empty computer lab. Although he called me once or twice to tell me not to come, my ride often arrived and I was on my way to campus before the phone rang!

Finally, my completed course work allowed me to take the first half of the psychology senior seminar. The purpose of the whole seminar involved researching, designing, and carrying out psychological research. This first half, taught by Dr. Maddox, focused on the literature review, finding or creating a survey for the method of gathering data, and designing the research experiment. The topic I chose to research involved measuring undergraduates' attitudes toward people with disabilities. I selected variables that I felt might affect attitudes included gender, years of higher education, major, and whether an individual had a family member or friend with a disability. Writing the majority of the paper in the summer gave me the additional time I needed.

By now, my physical stamina for typing papers had definitely increased. In my final fall quarter, I took the second half of the seminar with Dr. Johnson and two other courses. I didn't ask for accommodations because I did not anticipate needing any. Senior seminar only met weekly, and the second half students did not attend every class. Instead, we cruised around campus, looking for fellow undergraduates to complete our surveys. I used my connections to professors to enter their courses at the end of class to force students to fill out my survey. I hung out at the student center, too, particularly looking for guys to participate in my research. Since my survey was a questionnaire written in the '70s, I changed some of the wording to reflect "politically correct" language. To say that individuals with disabilities are not normal is, well, abnormal! Atypical, yes, but not abnormal.

My hard work paid off, with the 'A' that I received from Dr. Johnson, whom students thought should teach English as well as psychology. The professor asked me to participate in the research symposium the following spring. Over three days, a poster board I created highlighting my research project was displayed on campus. With colored paper in my computer's printer, I printed the project title, section subtitles, method, and findings in large, boldfaced font. Mom and I wanted the display to reflect my abilities. Except for assistance with gluing, it did. I even transported it on MetroLift and across campus myself – Dr. Johnson got stuck in traffic and didn't arrive on time to help me! The first day of the symposium, the students stood or sat, as Dr. Wilson suggested for me, by their projects and discussed them with students and professors.

Throughout the experience, I privately wondered what my research findings would have shown if I had conducted the project with faculty members as participants. Particularly if I had done so three years earlier.

***

My last spring quarter became memorable for yet another reason. Out of the blue, I received an email on my school account asking me to meet Dr. Michalos and Dr. Wilson in his office. I thought I did something wrong although, I couldn't imagine what, or I thought they were both reviewing my writing portfolio, a compilation of my work required for graduation. Since I hadn't yet had Dr. Wilson as a professor, his presence in this meeting really confused me.

Dr. Wilson was returning from class, as he pushed his storage cart. As I pushed my wheels, he held the door to the professors' offices, and I followed him into his space. I moved my walker out of the way of the entrance while we waited for Dr. Michalos. I think Dr. Wilson enjoyed watching me, quiet and a little uncomfortable, wondering why I was there.

Dr. Michalos came and sat down, asking her colleague if he told me yet. When he said he didn't, she finally informed me.

"Each year, faculty and staff members nominate students who have shown dedication to their education while involving themselves in the community or dealing with personal challenges. When we received our opportunity to nominate someone this year, both of us thought of you. We are nominating you as one of our 'Heroes of the University.' We will celebrate your award in May."

I started crying. What an honor! I had a difficult time listening to the details of the gathering that would take place a few weeks later. Both professors encouraged me to invite my mom and whomever else I wanted to include.

A few weeks later, Mom drove me to school, where we met Cris and my year old nephew, Carson. Cris was afraid to bring the baby, but I laughed seeing Dr. Hodo scoot Carson's toy train to him on the table as the retiring president passed us!

I was one of the last six students to stand up as Drs. Michalos and Wilson came over to me. The professor I had in class read as Dr. Wilson stood next to her.

"It would be easy to nominate Stephanie as a 'Hero of the University' because of her disability. That is not the reason for the nomination. Rather, Stephanie treats each of her assignments as a challenge to be met, not an obstacle to be overcome. We congratulate Stephanie with this award."

I hugged Dr. Michalos and shook Dr. Wilson's hand. Dr. Michalos mentioned going to lunch with me and Mom before my graduation. I laughed as I listened to the two women talking in their native New York accents.

***

One final course. While many of my friends graduated in May 2006, I had one more psychology elective left to take. Social Psychology met Monday through Thursday for five weeks. Then, I would graduate five weeks later during the August graduation ceremony. I took another class from the professor who was listed as the course instructor, so I felt comfortable walking into the classroom the first day. All of us were surprised, however, when a substitute came in and said the professor changed her mind. We needed a professor to teach the course. That day, we watched a film. I thought this could only happen in my final undergraduate class.

The second day of class, I walked into the classroom without a professor. I worried that the class would be cancelled. My worry quickly turned to relief and surprise when Dr. Wilson strolled in with his cart. Finally, I had the opportunity to take a course from one of my campus supporters. When I presented my accommodations letter and asked him if I needed to see the disability coordinator, he laughed and said, "No. You won't need many accommodations."

What a great class! We worked on group activities and had many interesting discussions. When we worked on individual in-class assignments, Dr. Wilson asked if I could circle multiple choice answers. I said I could if my paper was taped to the table, but I admitted to him that this would embarrass me. When he asked if participating without answering on paper would embarrass me, I shook my head.

That's what we did, and I joined the discussion without difficulties.

On an exam, Dr. Wilson accidentally marked one of my correct answers incorrect. Although he said someone else graded it, he asked me to explain my answer. I did, and he kept encouraging me to give him more information (it was a multiple-choice test). After several minutes of explaining, the professor smiled and credited my points.

***

August 19, 2006 became a highly anticipated day, six years in the making. With announcements sent, graduation gowns tried on, and a luncheon planned, Cris, Chad, my nieces and nephew, along with the entire Farrell family, attended the ceremony. Terry, Joe, Laurie, and her daughter Madeleine came from San Antonio. Dr. Russell, Dr. Botson, and Mrs. Botson, joined the celebration, too.

Mom drove me to campus early. On the sweltering day, the sky grew darker and darker as we rushed to the side of campus that hadn't been my territory in the past three years. Mom went ahead to the gym as I waited with the other graduates.

I did not want to use my walker that day, and I didn't. Still, on one of the most exciting days of my life, I didn't want to fall on stage. Mom already told me she was going to talk to the registrar, who coordinated the ceremony, about our options. With an hour until the beginning of the ceremony, I became anxious and began wondering what was going to happen. As graduates continued to arrive, the registrar found me and told me I would be accompanied by a staff member up the ramp and onto the stage. He would step away as my picture was taken. Before students began walking to the gym, Dr. Michalos came in and said the pouring rain brought the Greeks good luck. Little did we know that the lights went out in the gym!

The moment came to proceed to the gymnasium. The heavy rain stopped, leaving more humidity. Walking slowly in line to the gym, the graduates saw professors in their robes, too. I heard my Business Ethics professor call out to me and wave. I concentrated on walking and finding my seat in the long row. Looking over my shoulder, my family and friends gave me a 'thumbs up' sign. I don't remember a word of the commencement address. All I recall is a classmate behind me pushing down the cap on my constantly moving head!

My escort appeared when the last names beginning with 'T' began being called. As we walked, with my arm around his, I found myself following my sister and younger niece as they rushed to the restroom! In what seemed longer than a few minutes, the two of us walked up the steep ramp. After my name was called, with the accolade magna cum laude after it, I accepted my diploma from Dr. Michalos. Dr. Wilson was among those on stage, too. Walking with the escort back to my seat, I noticed tears streaming down Mom's cheeks.

The ceremony ended. Through the crowd, I hurriedly found Mom, who unzipped my robe to cool me off and helped me freshen up in the restroom. We then found our group, hugged, and took pictures. About forty five minutes later, everyone met in a private room at an Italian restaurant. I laughed at the cake my sister ordered, which read, "Way to go, Stephanie!"

Yes, I did go a long way.

12
Life after the Classroom: Accepting Reality, Wanting More

While Mom encouraged me to take time to relax and enjoy my accomplishments, I immediately began thinking about what to do next. My goal seemed simple - I wanted to work. Landing a job as an individual with a disability, college graduate or not, however, wasn't simple at all. In my continuing interest and research in disability-related topics, I was well aware of the extremely high unemployment rate of individuals with disabilities. I didn't need statistics, though, to inform me that employers saw and heard my impairments first, and then noticed my abilities – if they took time to reach that point.

Whatever worked out for me in the following months, or years, Mom wanted to be there for me as much as she could. After working most of her life, and mine, Mom decided to semi-retire. She continued to teach, substituting at the same private school one or two days a week. Additionally, Mom wanted to become my permanent caregiver, or at least get paid for my eleven hours per week I received from the state. Her caregiving time obviously required more than eleven hours, but now she would be compensated for that small portion of her time. I loved the idea. For over six years, I relied on too many caregivers coming in and out of our house. Now, Mom and I took care of my personal needs on our schedule. Best of all, I didn't need to train her!

***

As a client of DARS, I needed assistance in beginning my job search. I wasn't expecting miracles, nor did I expect anything to begin on a reasonable timetable. While I waited to meet yet another vocational rehabilitation counselor, I began to look for employment the best, and most independent way, I knew how – on the Internet. In addition to searching for specific jobs, I researched job descriptions, job accommodations, and organizations that might help in any way.

Within a week or two of graduation, I logged onto the website of United Cerebral Palsy (UCP) of Greater Houston. I had never been a client of UCP, as the organization mostly provided early intervention services and adapted toys for children. Although I learned of a weekly activities group for adults, I had little interest in doing arts and crafts. The support I needed and wanted involved using my knowledge and abilities. Pressing my MouseKeys and tapping on the "Jobs" page, I browsed the few listings and found one for a position entitled "Administrative Assistant."

The description listed the job as full time, which I knew I could not physically handle. I continued reading, though, and saw that the position included computer work I could certainly accomplish. Some duties involved fundraising activities, and while the job description didn't specify them, I hoped to find out. Copying her email address, I drafted a message to the contact person, attached my updated resume, and hoped for the best.

One or two days later, I received a response to my email asking me to call UCP for an interview. I wasn't sure disclosing my disability in my initial email was proper protocol, but I did it anyway. I didn't want my voice on the phone to be the first signal that I had CP. With my disability disclosed, and with a total lack of self-confidence, I called and scheduled an interview.

UCP's office was located by Cris' house, about a half of an hour's drive from our townhome. While that distance worried me in getting to and from the job if I was hired, I tried to concentrate on the immediate appointment. Mom drove me in my skirt and cardigan to the interview. Although my outfit was appropriate, my size two skirt shifted around my waist and caused my blouse to come untucked. Riding the elevator and locating the correct office, I felt sloppy, anxious, and perspiring. I imagined how the make-up I applied so carefully looked on my face as beads of perspiration appeared.

Finding the office and opening the accessible door, I gave my name to the receptionist and sat down in the waiting area. In my stiff, fisted right hand, I nervously clutched the leather straps of my black bag. The few minutes I waited didn't slow my breathing or stop my negative thoughts about what might happen in the interview. A woman then appeared, acknowledging me and asking me to follow her. I struggled to stand up and finally got my balance in my black flats. With my bag still clenched in my right fist, I tried to concentrate on walking straight and slowly.

In the small office, I took a seat in one of two chairs in front of a large desk. The woman mentioned that we were waiting for someone else to join us. When a younger woman entered the office, closed the door, and took the seat to the left of me, the interviewer introduced both of them and said something about my recent graduation from college.

"Yes, I just graduated from HBU." Not seeing my resume on her desk, I bent down to get my new, brown leather folder. Without a surface to place the folder on, I had great difficulties balancing it on my lap, opening it, and taking out a copy of my qualifications. During the several minutes it took me to do this, the young woman next to me whispered to the woman behind the desk.

"Should I help her?"

I felt like crying in frustration, *"No, I want to prove to you that I can do it."*

Finally, I took the paper out and handed it to the interviewer. Glancing at it, she asked me an unexpected question.

"Stephanie, are you from Houston?"

I answered her briefly, not understanding what my birthplace had to do with the job interview. She then asked me how I used the computer. After I described my keyguard and trackball, she said that their accountant, who also had CP, used a keyguard.

"I use word prediction software to increase my typing speed, too."

She had never heard of the software and jotted it down on a sticky note next to her computer.

"Well, the position requires some setting up for fundraising events, and sometimes we're at Reliant Stadium until late at night. We obviously wouldn't ask you to do that. We enjoyed meeting you."

Twenty minutes after Mom had dropped me in front of the building, I called her on a phone I asked to use in another office. She had just ordered a drink at Starbucks and was surprised to hear from me so soon.

Five minutes later, I sat in Mom's car, sipping a frappuccino in between telling her what happened during my non-interview.

"Don't let this discourage you. You're only starting to look for a job. You have to keep going."

I already felt discouraged, but I knew Mom was right. I didn't know, though, how long I needed to avoid discouragement.

***

The time came to meet my new VR counselor. Over eight years went by since I requested assistance as a job seeker. Although I now held a bachelor's degree, my awful experience at UCP confirmed that my obvious limitations would come into focus before my educational achievements.

Seeing my new counselor, a young man in a wheelchair, gave me hope that he identified with a few of the obstacles I encountered. As I should have known, however, I shouldn't have assumed anything - especially with my history at DARS.

Sitting next to his desk and briefly informing him of my background, I developed the impression Philip was indeed a new counselor. He didn't seem to know the correct procedures for helping me begin a job search. His lack of experience became more evident as we began to discuss what type of employment I sought.

"So, do you want to work in an office filing papers?"

"No, I physically couldn't do that for any length of time. I want to utilize my writing skills on the computer."

We established that I needed to choose an employment provider to work with me in my job search. I didn't want to randomly pick one from the list of providers he gave me, nor could I call them, ask questions, and note their responses. At home, I researched some of the providers on the Internet, but didn't find much information. So, I called Philip and asked if he could obtain some of their email addresses. He had difficulties understanding my speech on the phone, and didn't seem to understand the purpose of researching which provider I chose. He didn't always answer my email, either.

I called Karen at Advocacy.

***

Karen joined me when I next met with Philip. She supported my decision to research employment providers and offered some recommendations. My advocate also confirmed that I wasn't required to work full time to receive assistance with my job search.

After emailing numerous providers and receiving few responses, I chose one of Karen's recommendations to help me in obtaining employment. In a follow-up email, Norine invited me to a conference in which a leading author and disability employment specialist was going to speak. She thought the presentation would provide me with information and give us a chance to meet. With the event held in the early evening and somewhat far from home, Mom agreed to drive me.

Listening to the man offer examples of accommodating employees with disabilities, I began to feel excluded. Most, if not all, of the scenarios he described involved individuals with intellectual disabilities who could perform simple jobs. He explained how jobs could fit people who had capabilities in greeting customers at a superstore, or watering plants at a home gardening center. Mom and I kept glancing at each other. The expert's discussion didn't address any of my abilities, or my obstacles. When he welcomed questions from the audience, I really wanted to ask him about the circumstances he failed to discuss. Mom dissuaded me from doing so. She figured I wouldn't stop talking once I started!

When the small crowd began to mingle, I needed to somehow locate Norine. I was glad to spot Karen a few tables over, and went to talk to her. Norine hadn't been able to come. Karen introduced me to Kim, who worked for Norine. Kim, Karen, Mom, and I spoke for a few minutes. I gave her my resume and she said she would contact me.

A week later, Kim and a new colleague were sitting in our living room, getting to know me. Mom was home, but agreed to keep busy and let me do my own talking. Kim began by telling me a little about herself and her role in assisting individuals searching for employment. Her colleague did the same. When Kim described some of the jobs that she recently helped clients find and start, Mom walked in from the kitchen.

"Kim, those jobs sound appropriate for those clients. Stephanie graduated magna cum laude from college. She doesn't want to work in a garden. She needs to be intellectually stimulated."

I appreciated Mom's words on my behalf. Looking at her with piercing eyes, however, I asked her to find something to do!

"My mom is correct, though. We were both disappointed in listening to the speaker the other night. The types of employment and accommodations he discussed didn't relate to me. He failed to describe any type of scenario with an employee who has physical disabilities, particularly one with a college degree."

"I realized that, and I could tell you were disappointed. So, let's talk about you. You gave me your resume. Tell me more about yourself and what you want to do."

I thought I was being interviewed, but I wasn't really nervous. I spoke about my experiences at the community college and working for Dr. Russell. Moving on to HBU, I described how hard I worked, what types of accommodations I needed, and how I developed my writing skills. Both women looked through my writing portfolio.

"May I take this folder with me and have these assignments bound in one booklet? It will be easier to pass around to contacts and potential employers," Kim asked.

"Sure."

Kim explained that, in the coming weeks, her job involved getting to know me. Everything about me – my skills, my abilities, my challenges, my ideal employment specifications, and anything else that would help her help me gain employment. She wanted to accomplish this out in the community. When she mentioned going out to lunch, I told Kim I had trouble eating and conversing at the same time. I become so busy talking, I forget to eat, and vice versa.

Offering a suggestion, I said, "I enjoy going out for coffee." She confirmed where I liked to go.

"I'll pick you up next week and we'll head to Starbucks," Kim said.

***

Kim and I went to Starbucks once a week for many weeks. Essentially, she needed to complete the first of several reports about me, answering questions about the type of employment I wanted, job accommodations, the hours and setting I preferred, and other job-related needs and preferences. Discussing these specifications, I continually referred to my job as a work-study student. This was the last job I held, and more importantly, everything about it seemed ideal. I felt comfortable in a small and a very supportive environment, with somewhat varied tasks and feedback.

Once Kim completed the first report, which she asked me to proofread, the two of us, along with Karen, met with Philip. We discussed what we had done so far, and what activities we needed to accomplish to continue my job search. At this point, Karen knew Kim would encourage and support my best interests, so I agreed with Karen that her involvement in my case should end. I knew I could contact her again at any time.

Throughout this process, Kim relied on my Internet skills to research specific job titles and possible job leads. My employment provider continued to highlight the importance of networking. Although I thought of a few contacts from HBU, those who I reached out to before graduation, including the career counselor, never followed through with assistance. Still, I promised Kim I would follow up and contact them again. We continued exploring my network of former professors and neighbors.

"My mom and I have begun going out to dinner with a group of neighbors to celebrate our birthdays. Most of them are retired, though. I think one man in our birthday club is on a few organizations' boards."

I promised I would ask next time I saw him. Asking in person was easy. Networking on the phone, however, was a different matter. Kim agreed with me about not calling unfamiliar contacts. I didn't want to talk to people who didn't know me or my impaired speech patterns, at least not initially on the phone. So, Kim and I agreed that I would continue "e-networking," through email. She asked me to draft a few messages to send to organizations that interested me and any other contacts or possible links I found. All of this research kept me occupied.

Identifying possible employers close to my home, one company stood out in particular. Exactly five minutes across the beltway, this large software corporation was headed by an MBA graduate of HBU. I found myself wondering how I could make our two paths cross, though I never figured out how to make it happen. Checking the company's website every few weeks, I spotted the perfect position for me – a part-time, paid internship in the communications department. The job mostly included writing assignments and was designed for a current college student. I hoped that already having a degree would give me an advantage, and I quickly emailed the link to Kim. She encouraged me to complete the online application immediately.

A few weeks later, I received an unexpected call from the human resources department. Trying to control my anxiety, and excitement, I spoke as clearly as possible and answered questions succinctly. I knew, however, the first impression I made on the phone didn't reveal my best abilities.

The link to the job posting was deleted soon after the call. My obvious disappointment led my mom to tell me she didn't think such a large company would have been a good match for me. I agreed with her; but I mourned what seemed like an ideal opportunity.
***

As my primary contact to employment leads, Kim began inviting me to various seminars and events involving individuals with disabilities. Either with Kim or alone, I attended breakfasts with business leaders employing the disabled, discussions about job accommodations, and award ceremonies honoring those who made a difference in our community. While I enjoyed attending such events and learned some information, I continued to feel as if I was a minority in a minority. The individuals with disabilities I saw used wheelchairs. They had good fine motor abilities and typical speech. Many were already employed.

On a hot morning in May, I went to a ceremony celebrating an accessible playground in Memorial Park. Representatives from the National Council on Disability attended to honor Houston, or more specifically, the Houston Mayor's Office for People with Disabilities (MOPD). I took MetroLift and, as asked, represented Norine's organization. Standing up in the crowd before the ceremony, then-mayor Bill White shook my hand as he walked the center pathway in front of the new playground. As the ceremony began, the Executive Director of the MOPD, herself in a wheelchair, accepted the honor and spoke of the city's achievements, and those still needed, in providing access to the disabled community.

After the ceremony, waiting for my ride in the heat, I thought about my circumstances. As I saw the Executive Director at other functions, too, I quickly realized the determination and dedication it took her to reach that important position. Yet, I couldn't help but feel that her representation of individuals with disabilities didn't represent me, and many others. Perhaps I was envious of her abilities; I certainly felt jealous of her ability to drive off in her Mini Cooper, the car I would own if I could drive! My feelings went beyond wishing I didn't have the impairments I long ago accepted. Where exactly did someone with my limitations, and others with more severe challenges, fit into a society that wasn't always accessible or accommodating? When were improvements in accessibility in the adult world – in independent living, in transportation, in employment – going to be made for us?
***

My e-networking continued with messages sent to various organizations as I sought information about types of employment and job functions, or any request that might lead my crooked foot in the door. While some contacts kindly replied with wishes of luck, though no specific assistance to offer, most of my email went unanswered. Kim joined me a few times on phone calls when email didn't work. Once, I spoke to the director of an organization that disseminated all types of information to people with disabilities. At the kitchen table, Kim sat silently as I talked to the nationally known disability-rights activist. Scribbling ideas and questions on a legal pad, Kim encouraged me to speak slowly while emphasizing my skills and abilities. Although the man complemented me on my achievements, and my speech, he didn't have any opportunities to offer.

During one of my e-networking sessions, I found the name of a neurologist my parents took me to see while I was in high school. At the time, I remember a cool, quirky doctor who primarily gave my parents educational advice and provided a sympathetic ear while listening to all of our struggles regarding school. Dr. Silvers and my dad worked together on some computer projects. Since seeing him at my father's funeral, I knew he closed his practice and opened a clinic specializing in teaching literacy skills to students with severe reading challenges.

I tailored one of my email messages to the doctor who was familiar with my circumstances. Receiving a quick response, I finally had a job lead.

***

Dr. Silvers and I met the following week. The reading institute wasn't far from home, and offered a small (actually intimate) environment. I practiced the interviewing skills Kim and I had been rehearsing. My ever-present nervousness eased somewhat as I remembered I knew this man, and as a former neurologist, he understood my disabilities and would see my abilities. The interview didn't happen as I expected, however, as Dr. Silvers tested a student while speaking with me. Getting up every few minutes to check on the student, he told me he needed someone to write educational passages for him. At the end of the brief meeting, the doctor basically offered me a job if I wanted it!

I quickly shared my excitement with Kim, and we arranged to see Dr. Silvers together to discuss job specifics. Although Dr. Silvers offered to let me telecommute, I wanted to go into the workplace. After nearly a year of spending much of my time at home, I missed having somewhere to go. With less than twenty hours of work per week, I asked the doctor if I could come to work three days. He agreed. During our meeting, however, Kim and I did not hear any specifics concerning my position. While he gave us interesting information about students with reading difficulties and instructional methods that helped improve literacy skills, most of his information didn't apply to me. From what I gathered during the interview, my job involved researching and writing for children, not teaching them.

I brought my extra computer hardware and software with me – the keyboard with the keyguard, the trackball, and the word prediction program. Kim and I both left feeling overloaded with information, but I still had questions. Was I going to work in one of the smaller rooms behind the main room, which was divided into several areas for tutoring students? Would Dr. Silvers give me specific instructions on my first day?

***

I woke up early on the July day I had hoped – and worked for – to come. Feeling overdressed in my short-sleeved dress, I prayed my MetroLift ride arrived on time. After Mom put the finishing touches on my best appearance, I ate breakfast, and my ride finally came. Ten minutes later, I walked into the reading clinic with a black leather bag on my arm. Unsure of where to go, I wandered around a few moments until Dr. Silvers saw me and pointed me to one of the two smaller, back rooms. My computer equipment had been attached to a system in the far left corner of the room. I would sit parallel to a window. Looking around my new work environment, I suddenly realized just how tiny it was. The table in the center nearly backed up to my chair. I wouldn't have known where to park my walker if I brought it. A box between the window and my chair held my bag.

Still unsure of my first work task, I adjusted my keyboard on the table, placing blue Dycem beneath it to prevent sliding. The table lacked much work surface, so nothing would slide too far. My trackball needed to be moved to my left, but I felt too clumsy to do that myself. I began working on the computer, adjusting the accessibility features I needed. Dr. Silvers finally came in with a book and described the short, cause and effect passages he wanted me to write. He said I could write compare and contrast, too. The doctor had all levels of books I could use.

Just as I became familiar with the material and decided what I should begin writing, Dr. Silvers entered the room again, this time with a child and a parent. Closing the door behind them, the doctor sat down at the table behind me and began a tutoring session. I was glad he couldn't see my face; the proximity of three people in the room astonished me. My new job would be performed while listening to, and trying to tune out, the boss's voice instructing a child on how to read and coaching the parent on how to practice at home.

After two hours of work, I needed to eat the small lunch I brought. Although my hours were part-time, my energy expenditure required me to eat every few hours. With the three of them in the middle of a session, I tried to quietly leave the room. Dr. Silvers looked up at me and asked, "Are you leaving?"

I nervously responded, "I'm going to eat my lunch."

Before he repeated the question, I could tell he didn't understand me. I simply replied "no."

In the twenty minutes I took to eat, the student and his parent left. I figured I better return and settle into my work before another group joined me. When I was preparing to meet my ride home, I again navigated myself out of the room with three people right there.

Five and a half hours after I left, I returned home and shared my day with Mom. Then, as promised, I called Kim and told her the same story. I expressed my surprise, as she did, in working in such a cramped space with tutoring sessions taking place directly behind me. I would see how Wednesday, my next workday, went.

The next work days, and weeks, served as a lesson in adjusting to a strange, difficult environment. If my boss wanted me to work from home, he didn't say it. Instead, I learned to adapt to my surroundings, taking restroom breaks (in the one restroom) between having students in the room, concentrating on my work amidst distractions, and hoping for some feedback without receiving any. I also learned that paychecks were sometimes late!

With all of my years of dealing with stares, I found it disconcerting, particularly at work, when a child looked at me and asked, "Why does she move like that?" Dr. Silvers quickly explained how different we all are, and told the student I worked for him as a writer. He told one kid he needed to concentrate so he could read what I wrote. *Yeah, kid, I thought, worry about your own difficulties!*

I eventually became acquainted with tutors, especially one who turned out to be a Silvers! One of the doctor's sons, Pierce, often worked at the computer to my left. He and I exchanged ideas and helped each other as needed. Pierce seemed to understand my needs, and used another space, if available, to work with a student.

Quickly, I went through the several books I was given to produce pages and pages of passages. I became

175

frustrated at the lack of feedback I received since I started the job. Even when the boss didn't seem busy, I felt intimidated to asked questions. When my ride was extremely late one afternoon, Dr. Silvers offered to drive me home. I felt funny having the boss give me a lift. I benefited in two ways, however. I got home, and more importantly, I had an opportunity to talk to him and receive some feedback.

The following week, my boss gave me new material to use. Dr. Silvers also held a meeting to discuss tutoring and some of the content he wanted my writing to expose. During this meeting, I realized why my boss intimidated me. The manner in which he spoke to other employees, one of whom kept asking for clarification, was quite stern, and frankly, rude. I would have felt quite uncomfortable, and my anxiety would have peaked, if I had been on the receiving end of some of his responses.

My anxiety, in fact, did go into high gear one day as I read from a spiral-bound book. Since I had little table surface to hold my materials, I folded the book in half. Stopping by my computer, he saw the book and said, "Don't fold this over like that. You'll ruin the binding." I thought he was joking. He wasn't. Kim and I discussed these minor issues. The more they added up, the more I questioned why I continued to go to work.

In the middle of my job at the reading clinic, I agreed to complete a short project for Norine. Having still not met her, Norine, through Kim, asked me to edit a document. I gladly accepted the opportunity and felt empowered, even if it was temporary, to go from one job to the next. Working on the project at home reminded me how convenient it was to work day or night, and have ample space to do so.

Although I kept sharing my frustrations with Kim, I continued to remain silent at work. I understood I could have worked from home to avoid my uncomfortable working conditions, but my unhappiness went beyond those. I found myself becoming bored with what I was asked to write. Dr. Silvers mentioned the possibility of my writing parent training materials at some point, but he wouldn't give me a definite go-ahead when I brought up the subject. How many short, expository passages could I write for certain reading levels?

My conflicting feelings about remaining in the job caused me more stress. I wanted to work and knew I was lucky to have a job. The position, however, didn't turn out as expected. Dr. Silvers did me a great favor by hiring me. My expectations, and his needs in an instructional writer, didn't seem to match.

An experience on a Friday afternoon confirmed what I felt I had to do. Enjoying some time without anyone else in the tiny room, I suddenly became startled as I heard Dr. Silvers and Pierce arguing. Their voices became louder and louder until I easily heard everything they said, or in Dr. Silvers' case, yelled. I couldn't believe what I heard. I wanted to go home as soon as possible. I thought about calling Mom to pick me up, but the phone was in the front office. My pick-up time eventually came, and I said nothing as I passed Dr. Silvers. Taking a quick glance at my boss's face, I think he forgot I was working in the back room. Walking out the door, I waited outside until my cab arrived.

On Monday, with Dr. Silvers out of the office, I left my letter of resignation for him. Two weeks later, I left my first post-college position - six months after I accepted it.
***

Guilt over leaving a paid position faded as I knew I had told the truth in my letter of resignation. I did have another opportunity - I just didn't know when it would start or how long it would last. Kim shared that Norine wanted to hire me to bolster membership in the state chapter of an organization for employment providers who worked with individuals with disabilities. As the volunteer president of the chapter, Norine hoped to increase interest in a much needed area – supported employment. Although the national organization was mostly comprised of supported employment providers, our goal involved recruiting anyone concerned with the employment of people with disabilities.

Norine and I finally met at a disability-related event that Kim and I attended together before Christmas. After the breakfast honoring advocates, the three of us discussed what I could do to increase attention and membership to the chapter. With less than ten members throughout the state, I had work ahead of me. I had high hopes in attracting attention and support for an issue in which I had intense, personal interest.

The three of us exchanged plenty of emails planning to launch a website. Although I wasn't the webmaster, with Kim's input, I planned and wrote the content. I also developed a monthly e-newsletter containing short articles about job accommodations and supports, updated information pertaining to employees with disabilities, and employment trends. Several months into the project, I sent my newsletter to hundreds of employment providers, vocational counselors, and anyone else who might have interest in the cause. My ever-present self-motivation served me well in learning what I needed to do, including participating in national conference calls with people who knew more about the field than I did. I cared deeply about my work in supporting those who assisted anyone with a disability become employed. The combination of my significant physical challenges and my intellectual abilities, however, made me feel as if I was a minority within a minority. The more research I did for my work, the more I felt my chances of finding permanent employment were becoming bleaker and bleaker.

All of my hard work and determination in growing the much-needed statewide organization failed in the end. The dwindling economy, the steep membership costs, and the lack of interest severely impacted any plans laid out or any efforts made to join people together. With only one or two new memberships, our chapter's budget ran out. I tried not to take it personally. After a year and a half of putting forth great effort, I faced unemployment again.

***

Kim kindly offered her assistance again in finding me employment. I didn't want to keep walking down that long, arduous road. With the information and job search techniques I acquired from my employment provider, I hit the Internet day after day looking for whatever I could find. A few weeks later, I landed on a website that hired online writers. I applied by submitting three sample articles, which I got paid to write. After being asked to rewrite one article, I wasn't hired. As disappointed as I was, I realized I could not produce the required twenty articles per month to remain a writer on the site.

If I found that website, I could find another, and I did. This time, I submitted an application one day and received a positive response the next. My acceptance as a writer led me to begin writing education articles aimed at elementary school parents. Once I developed the correct techniques and understood the provided guidelines, I expanded to expository articles for parents of children in special education, high school students, and undergraduates. Eventually, I joined other channels on the site and wrote about topics involving psychology. I didn't earn much income. I was, however, remaining productive and using the two majors I studied.

Months went by as I continued to write as many articles as possible. I developed a small online following and enjoyed receiving comments, both positive and negative, from people around the world. Although I periodically searched for other employment opportunities, I kept researching and writing. Soon, in August 2010, a year had passed from when my first published article appeared.

Then, on a typical summer morning, Mom's life – and mine - changed. Suddenly, I needed to help Mom keep her balance – and try to balance more issues I never imagined I would have to weigh.

13
Difficult Changes:
Making Decisions,
Accepting Choices

On a Tuesday morning in August 2010, I lay in bed watching TV until Mom came into my bedroom. She, and her ever-present furry companion Lily, sat on my bed as we talked. As she always did in the morning, Mom walked to my two windows and opened the blinds. Walking back from the windows, her left leg appeared weak and seemed to give out from under her. She quickly reached for the wrought iron frame of my bed.

"Mom, what's wrong?"

"I don't know. My leg feels funny. I can't get my balance on it."

"You better not try to walk down the stairs. Sit on your bottom and go down like I do."

I waited until my mom was downstairs and went down myself. As I helped Mom with breakfast, I worried about her compromised balance. She held onto the kitchen counters and table to avoid falling. I encouraged her to remain seated while I cleaned up after we ate.

A few hours passed before both of us realized Mom had to go to the doctor. I didn't know at the time that those few wasted hours would change both of our lives forever.

Mom somehow managed to get dressed with me coming in and out of her room to help her and offer suggestions on how to keep from falling. She called Dr. Ericson's office to tell them what was happening. The receptionist told her to come immediately. Mom then called one of our neighbors and asked her to drive us.

The three of us sat in the half-full waiting room. Dr. Ericson's nurse opened the door and called Mom to an examining room. Although the nurse knew we had a close relationship, I could tell she didn't like me accompanying Mom into the room. I thought about telling her I wanted to be with Mom, but I didn't bother. She most likely wouldn't have understood me.

"They're both here," I heard the nurse say through the closed door before Dr. Ericson entered.

I sat and listened as the doctor asked my mom questions and helped her adjust her body on the examining table. As Dr. Ericson checked Mom's reflexes and asked her to perform certain physical tasks, I observed how much difficulty she now had in doing these exercises - almost as much as I did. Standing up without shoes, my mom nearly lost her balance a few times. With the doctor's assistance, she sat up on the table again.

"I don't think you have had a stroke. I think you may have Parkinson's disease. You need to see a neurologist."

Mom and I looked at each other as the doctor rattled off and jotted down names of neurologists he recommended. He also advised Mom to start walking with a cane.

Bending down, I turned Mom's shoes so that she could slip them on easily. Dr. Ericson chuckled and said, "This is quite the role reversal."

I laughed nervously. The role reversal was only beginning.

***

That night, Mom and I sat on her bed. We cried as we shared our worry in what was happening and what might happen. Mom shook her head and cried, "I wanted to be able to take care of you as long as possible."

"I know, but we'll have to take care of each other now."

***

The next couple of days were a blur as Mom called each of the recommended neurologists Dr. Ericson had given her. She could not schedule an appointment for two weeks, but was placed on a waiting list if a cancelation occurred. Meanwhile, until Cris bought a cane, I followed Mom everywhere. Although neighbors offered to walk Lily, the damn dog wouldn't go with anyone else but Mom. So, whenever Mom took her outside, I went with them. I don't know what I expected to do if Mom fell, but I had to be with her.

By the weekend, I felt more anxious and overwhelmed as Mom tried to follow her daily routine. One of our neighbors, who knew Dr. Ericson, called him and said she was worried about Mom and wondered if he could do anything else for her. I wondered what else was said and could be discussed during this conversation, but I was glad a friend was trying to advocate for my mom. Knowing this made me feel less alone.

I was alone, however. Cris and Chad enjoyed a mini-vacation in Mexico while I did my best to help Mom.

***

The phone rang Monday morning with news of a cancelled appointment with the neurologist. She could see the doctor that afternoon. Mom called our next-door neighbor, Nell, to see if she could drive us. She could.

"Are you going with us?" Mom asked me.

"Of course I am!"

After lunch, Mom, using her three-pronged cane, and I sat in Nell's car as she took us to Memorial City Medical Center. The three of us took the elevator to the second floor of the professional building and hiked the long distance to the neurologist's office. For what seemed like the first time in my life, I didn't need to try to keep up with Mom. Nell, at least ten years older than my mom at sixty-eight, and I walked slowly as Mom struggled to reach the office.

When we reached the beautifully decorated waiting room with lavender walls, Mom gave her name to the office manager, who handed her numerous forms to complete. Mom struggled to write, barely able to make check marks next to a long list of symptoms. I helped her get the list of her medications I typed, and took out her insurance cards from her wallet. She scribbled some information on the papers, doing her best. I felt her frustration and pain, knowing I couldn't write anything for her. As she tried to produce her once beautiful signature, I looked away to hide my sadness.

Once she gave the materials back to the office manager, we waited a few minutes until Mom was called into an examining room. I wanted to go with her, but Mom told me I should wait with Nell. Looking through the neurology magazines on a small table, I pretended to read as I tried to listen for any voices I could hear.

About twenty minutes later, the examining room door opened and I heard the doctor asking Mom to walk up and down the hallway. The female voice said something about Mom's left foot dropping and dragging. Before closing the door again, the doctor instructed Mom on how to better use her cane. A few minutes later, the door opened again and I heard Mom talking to the doctor at the front desk. I couldn't sit any longer; I stood and walked to the office window. Mom was standing with a relatively young, attractive physician with strawberry blonde hair.

"What's wrong, Mom?" I quietly asked through the opened glass-door window.

"Dr. Steinman thinks I had a stroke."

"A small one. One side of your lip is drooping. The MRI will tell us more," the doctor said. "Don't forget to start taking daily aspirin again."

"I thought you were taking aspirin every day, Mom."

"I stopped. Dr. Ericson said I had low cardiovascular risk."

The possibility of Mom having a stroke stunned me, and I began beating myself up. I thought I knew the symptoms of stroke. Mom's left leg weakness without other symptoms such as garbled speech and a headache didn't register that she had a stroke. If I realized it, I would have called 911. Of course, I wasn't a doctor, and in the coming months, I would learn more about medicine than I ever cared to know. Most of all, I learned that Mom's stroke was not very "small."

***

Cris called in the middle of her trip. I happened to be near the phone. Mom was in the bathroom; I didn't know if she wanted to tell her herself. I asked her if I could tell Cris, and she said "yes."

"The neurologist thinks Mom had a stroke. She's going for an MRI on Friday. Nell is driving us."

"She had a stroke!"

I didn't say much else because I didn't want to upset Mom. I told my sister that we would need her help when she returned from her trip.

***

The three of us piled into Nell's car again at the end of the week to go for Mom's MRI. On the way, Nell told us about the stroke she had in her forties. Her stroke resulted in aphasia, or the inability to speak, and other physical impairments. Nell's story gave me hope, as she recovered and resumed her teaching career.

After finding the correct suite where Mom was going to have the test, I accompanied her to the insurance desk. I wanted to support her emotionally, but I also didn't want her to forget anything. She seemed to need help answering questions, too. When the woman escorted Mom to a group of curtained off dressing rooms, I went with her. I couldn't provide much help, but I kept track of her clothes. Wearing a gown that someone else had to tie, Mom waited in an internal waiting room while I returned to Nell.

The hour that the test took dragged slowly. Nell and I always had a difficult time communicating with each other, so other than a few exchanged words, we didn't talk. Over an hour passed, and Nell and I both became antsy. I finally asked a woman at the front desk what was happening. She let me go back and wait in the internal waiting room where she said Mom would go when she was finished. After another twenty minutes or so, Mom came. She told me that she hadn't expected blood to be drawn to show images of her brain with and without contrast – whatever that meant. Mom looked tired; I went with her to the changing room and assisted her in getting dressed. While she went to the restroom, I went to tell Nell that we would leave in a few minutes.

Now, we had to wait for the neurologist to explain the results.

**

Cris took us to the next appointment with Dr. Steinman. Mom didn't want both of us going in with her, so I received the privilege of waiting for them. I encouraged Cris to take notes for both Mom and me. I needed to know any advice the doctor gave, since I had the responsibility of helping her, as she helped me, every day.

The appointment ended more quickly than I expected. Mom indeed had a stroke. Dr. Steinman wanted her to see a cardiologist, who would find where the blood clot originated. In the meantime, Mom needed to begin physical therapy to improve her balance and coordination. Since Mom hadn't driven in weeks, Dr. Steinman gave her the go-ahead to begin driving slowly, close to home. That worried me. Who else was going to drive us to the essential places we needed to go, though? With Cris living over twenty minutes away, caring for three school-aged children, her availability was limited.

**

Mom chose to have her physical therapy in Town & Country Village, the same shopping center where she worked years ago. Before she took herself to the initial appointment, she practiced driving around the townhome complex. I rode with her, and I saw how apprehensive she was behind the wheel. Mom had to concentrate on how to start the ignition and operate the car. As a non-driver, I tried to give her guidance, but my advice only seemed to interfere with her concentration.

"Stephanie, don't talk to me. I can't concentrate and listen you to at the same time."

So, I just sat in the passenger's seat and observed the road, trying not to allow my intense anxiety increase hers. As she started going to twice weekly PT sessions, I went along for the ride. Mom didn't want me going to therapy with her, and I didn't particularly want to watch, so she dropped me off at the Village. These trips became some of the first times I shopped by myself. While Mom tried to regain lost skills, I learned how to navigate entrances with heavy doors and ask for help with my wallet if I bought something.

"My PT asked me today how I got to therapy," Mom told me one day. "She doesn't think I should drive."

The fact that I went along with Mom on these trips, let alone allowed her to drive, astonishes me. At the time, I felt too scared and overwhelmed to know what else to do, or even to care, if we both got hurt in an accident.

***

The request of not talking to Mom while she was driving seemed to resonate in other, if not all, daily activities. Neither one of us liked a quiet house. We usually talked in between doing chores while watching TV or listening to music. As weeks passed after Mom's stroke, however, her cognitive impairments became more apparent. I couldn't help but notice her inabilities to tune out distractions. When I helped prepare dinner, for example, I had to lower the TV volume. We never went as far as turning it off; neither one of us would have liked that! If I stood next to her at the counter, though, I observed her struggle to decide what to do next. I often handed her the correct cooking utensils and tried to guide her through the process, all while limiting the words I spoke.

Mom had been my primary caregiver since I graduated from college. While I continued to do more and more to dress myself, do laundry, and perform other household chores, I still required a lot of assistance with certain tasks. Bathing was one of them. Mom couldn't bend down and wash me anymore. So, Cris began coming over once or twice a week to bathe me. She also started grocery shopping for us. I either emailed our list to her, or she took me to the store. I didn't realize going to the store with Cris began to prepare me for more independent shopping trips.

***

Three months after Mom's stroke, she and I went to lunch on the Monday before Thanksgiving. One of our favorite fast-food places to eat, the bagel shop was located in Town and Country Village, too. After lunch, we did our usual and walked the short distance to The Gap and looked around at the fall clothes. Although we regularly went on these mother-daughter outings, something about this one felt different. I figured out why. While I looked around the store, I kept an eye on Mom, making sure she didn't leave her cane anywhere or held onto merchandise she didn't want to buy.

I noticed the concentration and confusion on Mom's face as she started the car.

"Which pedal do I push for the brake?"

"Mom, you're asking a non-driver! It's the middle one."

I silently prayed that we would arrive home safely. We did, but I knew I had to immediately talk to Cris about stopping Mom from getting behind the wheel.

I never had to talk to Cris. That day turned out to be the last time Mom drove.

***

Mom and I usually took turns emptying the dishwasher at night. I had become pretty efficient at putting most of our cups and plates away while setting the breakfast table. That Monday night, Mom started the chore. As I watched TV in the living room, I heard the clanking of dishes, though more softly than if I was putting them in the cabinets. Then, I heard a hard thump. Hurrying into the kitchen, I saw Mom trying to sit up in the middle of the tiled floor.

"Mom, can you get up?"

"I don't know."

"I'm calling Cris."

I had to dial my sister's number many times to hit the correct buttons. When Cris answered, I quickly told her what happened.

"I'm going to slide a chair over to her to see if she can get herself up. Lily, get out of the way!"

Cris stayed on the phone while I advised Mom on how to use the kitchen chair to help pick her body up. Once Mom was safely seated, she talked to Cris on speaker. Nothing was hurting yet, so Cris asked if Mom thought she could go upstairs and get ready for bed.

"Call me if you need me," Cris said before I hung up the phone.

I wanted her to push herself up each step on her bottom, but Mom didn't think she could do that. So, she slowly walked up each step, tightly gripping the black banister. Waiting until she reached the top of the staircase, I followed her up with her cane and brought her nightgown to her. I helped her take off her pants as she sat on her bed. With her gown on, she went into the bathroom with her cane and washed her face and brushed her teeth. I stayed with her and watched as she struggled to stand up from the commode. After she lay down, I put the cane next to her bed.

"Promise you will call me if you have to get up during the night."

She promised. I went downstairs to turn off the lights. Upstairs again, I fought the temptation to just collapse on my bed before undressing. I checked on Mom one more time after I finished in the bathroom. My exhausted self finally hit the bed. After I prayed for Mom, I didn't sleep at all.

An hour or two later, I startled from a sound coming from Mom's bedroom. I quickly got up, walked through the dark hallway, and found Mom lying down outside her bathroom. She went to the bathroom and fell on the way back to bed. Lily circled her, not knowing what was happening.

"Mom, I told you to call me."

"I didn't want to. I had to go to the bathroom and did fine until I got here. I can't get up."

"I need to call Cris. And 911."

"No, you can't! It's the middle of the night and you can't wake the kids. I don't want to go to the hospital in the middle of the night."

"Mom, what are you going to do? Lie here all night?"

"I'll keep trying to get up. Listen to me, I don't want you to call anyone now."

"Okay. Can I help you try to get up?"

I didn't wait for an answer, but I couldn't do anything to help her. I put her pillow under her head. Against my better judgment, I went back to bed. I didn't sleep, though, getting up every hour to check on her. Except for moving a bit closer to the bed, she remained in the same position she managed to get into hours before.

Daylight finally came. I waited until 7:00 and checked on her one more time before telling Mom that I was calling Cris, then 911.

"I have to get dressed first!"

"Mom, you are on the floor. How are you going to dress yourself when you can't get up?" Before she responded, I walked to my room and dialed the phone.

As soon as Cris picked up the phone, I started rambling about what was happening. I said I was calling an ambulance after I hung up, and she should come over as soon as she possible. Then, I called 911. I tried to calm down because I was afraid they wouldn't understand me. I was relieved when the dispatcher confirmed our address. She began asking questions about Mom's status. Although she wanted me to stay on the line, I told her I needed to go downstairs, turn off our alarm, and unlock the door. I also wanted to call my neighbor.

"Mom, an ambulance is coming. I'm going down to call Don."

"Lily needs her breakfast."

"Mom, don't worry about the damn dog right now!"

As soon as I hung up the phone with Don, I opened the kitchen blinds and saw an ambulance passing back and forth on the street in front of our townhouse. As with MetroLift, the driver couldn't find our address. I hit redial on the phone and called Don again. He said he would go outside and direct them to the carport. I then ran around trying to lock Lily in the kitchen.

About fifteen minutes later, I sat in my nightgown, surrounded by Joyce, Don, and Arnold. I told Joyce that Mom was in her nightgown and had taken off her panties, so Joyce went upstairs and helped Mom put on some underwear. My neighbors and I watched two burly paramedics come through the back door with a gurney. Before going upstairs, one paramedic began asking questions about Mom. I started answering them, but the paramedic looked to Arnold.

"Listen to her. She knows everything you need to know," Arnold said.

The paramedics then went to get Mom. While they were upstairs, I started crying and babbling to Don and Arnold that I knew something like this could happen.

"I've been so nervous the past couple of weeks. Mom shouldn't have been driving; I thought we were going to be in an accident. I worried about her on the stairs. When she fell last night, and again during the night, I knew it was bad."

"Why didn't you call us, even in the middle of the night?"

"I don't know. I should have."

Mom came down on the stretcher and said 'hello' to our two neighbors. I told the paramedics that Mom's doctors practiced at Memorial City Hospital and they should take her to that ER. One of them asked if Mom took any medications.

"Yes, several. I don't have the list printed. It's on my computer."

"We need it."

My neighbors saw how shaky I was as I stood up. Joyce asked the paramedics if they could give me a lift up the stairs!

The next thing I knew, I was being carried upstairs as one guy held my arms, and the other held my legs. I tried to control my hand movements as I turned on my computer, found the file, and printed it. The two men waited on the stairs until I handed one of them the list. They carried me downstairs and I kissed Mom before they rolled her out to the ambulance.

"Now, we better get you and Lily some breakfast, then you should get dressed to be ready when Cris comes," Joyce said.

I'm glad someone was telling me what to do. I couldn't think through my anxiety, fear, and exhaustion.

***

Cris and I sat in a small room within the ER. Mom had been examined once and the doctor thought her left hip was broken. Cris was already planning for the future – both immediate and long-term.

"We should have moved the two of you right after the stroke. You can't go back to the townhouse; I'm going to start looking into assisted living places. Mom, you can't drive anymore."

"Can we deal with one issue at a time?" I didn't like my sister's comment about moving us, although I knew we couldn't continue living in the townhouse. While I was glad she told Mom that she couldn't drive again, I felt sad – for both of us.

"If I have to stay in the hospital for a while, where will Stephanie go?"

"She can stay with me," Cris said. "Do you mind if we go out to Tomball for Thanksgiving?"

I lied and said I didn't mind. Instead of having a small celebration at Cris and Chad's house, we were going to my brother-in-law's parents' home, forty minutes away. Although this was our tradition for the past couple of years, Mom didn't think she could be around so many people this Thanksgiving. It didn't matter now. She wasn't going anywhere, and I didn't want to think of celebrating.

***

We learned the certainty of Mom's broken hip a few hours later. Mom startled us, particularly Cris, with her confusion.

"Can't I wait and have surgery after the holidays?"

"Mom, your hip is broken. You won't be able to walk!"

She reminded us that she climbed the stairs last night. Cris and I tried to patiently explain that she would most likely have surgery that night. We couldn't stay any longer at the hospital, though. I needed to go home and pick up clothes and other essentials to last a few days. Cris was going to take Lily to the vet to board, since my nieces and nephew were afraid of her. Then, she had to go home to meet the kids from school. Saying goodbye to Mom, I had to control my emotions as I stood by her bed and noticed how small and frail she looked. The thought that I may not see her again crossed my overloaded mind.

***

I went to my sister's house and settled into my nephew's sports-themed bedroom. Carson didn't seem to mind lending his room to Aunt Stephanie for a while and sleeping with his younger sister. Cris asked Chad to put Carson's mattress on the floor because she was afraid I couldn't climb up on his high bed. I was more fearful of climbing their steep hardwood staircase. Just as I did at home, I limited my trips up and down the stairs. Climbing wood stairs instead of carpeted ones, with at least five more steps, tested my balance and stamina.

While I washed my face that night after a day that seemed like a week, I heard the phone ring. I cracked open the door and heard Chad talking. A few minutes after he hung up, he stood at the doorway and told me that Mom's surgery was over. The orthopedic surgeon said it went well. Knowing that good news, along with taking a diazepam, allowed me to relax into the slumber I so desperately needed, but thoughts of the changes ahead continued to drift in and out of my mind.

***

Visiting Mom in the hospital gave me something to do. Cris, on the other hand, had too much to do, and dropping me off to see Mom gave her some time to do them by herself. She already began researching retirement and independent living communities online and calling to inquire about rental prices. Since I couldn't use their computer without my assistive technology, I couldn't help. I did provide information about Mom's finances and the long-term care insurance. Cris, Chad, and I had some intense discussions at night, after the children went to bed. Many times, I felt decisions were being made for us.

195

Although I knew Mom couldn't make decisions then, I wanted a say in where I would live.

"Cris, I'm not going to live across town. All of Mom's doctors are at Memorial City."

"You may not have a choice. It depends on what you can afford. Most of these places have shuttle buses to take you to stores and doctors, anyway. Neither one of you can drive. "

"I know that! We also have friends in our neighborhood. I don't want to live in a totally unfamiliar area."

I realized Cris was trying to make good decisions in the middle of dire circumstances. Most nights, however, I went to bed feeling as though I was struggling to have my voice heard.

Since I couldn't do much of anything at Cris' house, I caught up on my phone calls. I first called Dr. Russell, whom I now called Nancy. She provided an empathetic ear and sound advice. I informed her of what had happened, and was comforted when she asked me to continue calling her – every day. Not surprisingly, she knew I needed someone to listen to me, and someone to remind me to manage one day, or one step, at a time.

I also called the home health care agency that paid Mom to care for me at the time, explaining my need for another provider. Contacting my state caseworker to obtain more weekly hours became a full time job, one that Cris would take on with me.

***

"I need to go home. I feel like I'm in the way here, and I want to start packing for our move," I explained to Cris and Chad during one of our nightly discussions after Thanksgiving. I didn't have any idea how long Mom would stay in rehabilitation, and I wanted to live in my home before moving.

"You're not in the way, and you can't go home by yourself," Chad said to me.

"Why not? I called my home health agency and they are looking for a provider for me, and Cris and I are trying to contact my caseworker. I'm calling her supervisor tomorrow. I know I will receive an increase in hours, and I'll get Advocacy involved if necessary."

"What happens if you fall? Arlene will never forgive Cris if something happens to you."

"Chad, I could easily fall going up and down your staircase. Having the girls walk behind me is even more dangerous, and it scares me. I'm used to my own stairs. Besides, I'm an adult."

"You are, but we're responsible for you while Arlene is in the hospital."

"What about when she goes to rehab? I can't stay here that long. I need to start cleaning out closets and packing. Who's going to do all of that?"

"You can go home only if Arlene agrees with it."

During my phone call to Mom the next day, I didn't beg for her permission. Rather, I told her she had to let me go home. I reminded her of neighbors who would help me if and when I needed it. I didn't give her any reasons to disagree with me, and she didn't.

* * *

Returning to the townhouse included more difficulties than I expected. The home health agency had a hard time finding reliable caregivers, which didn't surprise me. I felt the same vulnerability I experienced when I waited on providers to help me during college. This time, I felt it more acutely. I was reliant on a caregiver to make three meals a day. If a caregiver didn't arrive within fifteen minutes of her scheduled time, I began to worry.

As much as I felt alone, I wasn't. My neighbors surrounded me with support. Judy and Arnold, in particular, made daily visits to check on me and provide emotional support when I most needed to talk, or more often, to vent. With Arnold working from home, I knew I could always call him to prepare me a quick meal or clean up one of my many kitchen disasters if I couldn't do it myself. Most importantly, Judy and Arnold had both been through (and in Judy's case, continuing to go through) taking care of their elderly mothers. Wiping tears from my cheeks and listening to me describe my emotions, Judy and Arnold understood my difficult circumstances and acknowledged the feelings I was too overwhelmed to understand at the moment.

Starting to organize, discard, and pack more than four rooms of belongings pushed aside, at least temporarily, the emotional waves I was riding. I used my fear, anxiety, and anger in clearing closets and drawers. In the midst of finding reliable caregivers, the agency accused me of using providers to assist me in packing. Of course I had them help me do some of the things I couldn't do, especially when one sat on the couch while I was on the floor sorting and packing books. I didn't, however, ask anyone to do anything that would hurt her or overstep the boundary of providing much needed assistance at an overwhelming time.

***

Cris certainly felt overwhelmed, too, as she began visiting retirement communities and independent living complexes. She had several complicated decisions to make, and her stress level was understandably extreme. So much so that during one of our multiple, and quick, daily phone exchanges, she mentioned our cousin Laurie's email and offer for me to go to San Antonio, or for her to come to Houston.

"I may need you to go to San Antonio for a while because there's too much going on here."

198

"Cris, I'm not going anywhere. I already miss Mom so much and I want to visit her in rehab. And, I want to pack as much as I can."

I was hurt that Cris thought I should leave town. I realized, though, I needed more help and support to deal with everything. Although I hadn't seen her since my college graduation, and I felt nervous talking to her on the phone after so long, I called Laurie immediately.

"Laurie, I think I'm going to have to take you up on your offer. I don't want to leave, though."

"I realized you probably wouldn't want to come here. I was planning on coming to you before you called. I'll see you on Friday!"

Laurie spent four days with me over each of the next two weekends. I was nervous seeing my favorite cousin after two years of little contact. I shouldn't have been; Laurie and I easily caught up on each other's lives and shared a lot of fun in the middle of chaos. She assisted enormously, too, bringing boxes, weeding out non-essentials in the kitchen (a daunting task that baffled me), starting to pack, and driving me to visit Mom. Even as she preoccupied herself with my mom's books about Princess Grace while I cleaned out the hall closet, her company motivated me.

"I guess I'm not helping much by sitting and looking at books!"

"No, not really! That's okay; just having you here helps. Did you know Mom named me after Princess Grace's wild-child daughter, Stephanie? The doctor who delivered me was supposedly a distant relative of the Grimaldis of Monaco."

***

In between Laurie's visits, Cris took me on a tour of The Terrace, an independent living retirement community just ten minutes from the townhouse. Mom and I would share a one-bedroom apartment with a living room, dining area, and a tiny kitchen in total of 680 square feet. The advantages of living there included breakfast and lunch served on weekdays in the dining room, and a shuttle bus running on weekdays and Saturdays for trips within a certain distance of the community. The primary advantage I saw in living at The Terrace involved the shopping center next door - Memorial City Mall. In fact, the woman giving us the tour mentioned that I could go to the mall almost any time I wanted to go. Maybe to window shop after we pay our rent, I thought!

When I asked the woman if any younger people lived in the community, she mentioned one or two names of individuals who lived with their mothers. I cringed, however, when she said I could easily remain living there for thirty or forty years. Again, I experienced a pang in my stomach as I felt decisions were being forced upon me. Aside from the tremendous expense, I hardly wanted to consider spending the rest of my life surrounded by old people.

I agreed to give this living arrangement a year, and stamped my signature on the lease. Over the next weekend, I showed Laurie our new home. She optimistically thought it could work. Judy, whose mother had once lived there, suggested that I think of it as an adventure, like sharing a dorm room. On a rainy, January day, I reluctantly moved into The Terrace, a few days before Mom was released from rehabilitation. Although I knew I would see my former neighbors again, my new home seemed worlds away from anyone, or anywhere, familiar.

14
Role Reversal: Providing Care, Caring for Myself

Waking up that first morning at The Terrace, I looked forward to seeing Arnold, who already told me that he would meet me for breakfast in my new community. I realized as I dressed myself how tight our living space would be once Mom arrived. Arnold knocked on the door and together we walked the short distance to the dining room.

Sitting at the "New Residents" table, I looked around at all of the old faces, and the numerous walkers parked around the perimeter of the room. My summers with Nana made me comfortable around older people. I certainly was used to seeing the equipment of disability – the walkers and wheelchairs I used on and off over the years, and what I saw other students use in high school. Living at The Terrace combined these two factors, and many more, to the extreme. Eating breakfast, Arnold and I didn't know which was funnier, us looking at them, or their continuous glances at us. He joked that we should tell my new neighbors that he was my sugar daddy!

At lunchtime, I went to the dining room by myself. Although the executive director knew I was moving in with my mother, he apparently didn't remember this when he saw me. Preparing to eat alone at the table, I needed help mixing sugar in my iced tea and cutting my food. As a few people joined me at the table, my awkwardness increased. They didn't understand my speech nor did they understand why someone my age ate there alone. Frankly, I didn't understand the situation either.

A woman with short, white hair came and sat down next to me. We began talking, and she listened carefully as I told her my story. At eighty-seven, Adaline befriended me, helped me, and took the time to get to know me - and Mom. Having once known a coworker with CP, and having a granddaughter with a disability, Adaline understood I was more than my disability.

***

Cris brought Mom to her new home two days later. Seeing the tiny apartment, rather than the floor plan we showed her, shocked her. My sister and brother-in-law did a decent job of arranging our living room furniture and Mom's accent pieces. Although Mom's Asian screen divided our couch from my computer workstation, our living area was tight. The bedroom with double beds and one walk-in closet looked even smaller. If Mom and I weren't close now, we sure would be after this arrangement.

Mom's presence in our new home made me happy because almost two months had passed since we had been together every day. Her arrival also made me sad and anxious. Always petite, Mom lost more than ten pounds in rehabilitation. She now walked with a walker to keep her balance, had difficulties with fine motor skills, and was dealing with vascular dementia. I later learned her tremors were a result of vascular Parkinson's Disease. We both had to cope with many new changes and challenges.

As Mom and I lay in our beds those first few nights, she told me how she wanted to go home.

"I don't like it here. I'm too young to live here. We need to go home."

"You're too young to live here! What about me? I feel like a kid compared to all of these old people. We can't go home, Mom. You cannot manage the townhouse, and you'll receive physical therapy here. I don't like it here either, but I agreed to give it a try. You need to do the same."

Mom and I had many more discussions, actually arguments, over weeks and months until we both reached a breaking point.

***

Breakfast was served too early for Mom to get ready and go to the dining room, so we usually ate in the apartment. Once a week, I woke up and dressed myself to go to the dining room alone. I sat with Adaline and her friends, Maxine and Norman. The three of them offered assistance and support when I needed it. Still, walking into the room each day, even with Mom at lunch, made me feel more different than I ever felt. Being asked my name repeatedly by the same individuals, experiencing communication difficulties due to their hearing problems and my speech impairment, and having others tell me I was too young to live at The Terrace grew old quickly!

One convenience I enjoyed at our new home involved taking the shuttle bus. With pick-ups every hour on weekdays and Saturdays, the shuttle could take me places within a certain distance of The Terrace. Now that I had the responsibility of grocery shopping, I asked my caregiver to meet and assist me at the store. At least once a week, however, I went somewhere on my own. Increasing my independence and confidence, these trips provided me time to myself away from an extremely cramped environment. The young female driver and I became fast friends. Like Adaline, she saw beyond my disability, and she empathized with me. I laughed as she told tell me I was one of her only passengers without hearing difficulties. Many times, I stayed on the bus while she picked up other passengers to have more time to myself.

When Mom felt like going with me, we went out to lunch or went shopping. As much as I wanted these outings to remind me of our former life together, they highlighted the differences now. I certainly became accustomed to being as careful as possible to limit my falls. Now, I needed to watch out for Mom to prevent her from falling. I also had to help her keep track of her walker, purse, or anything else she might leave behind.

***

If a few incidents made me laugh, although nervously, throughout these months, they were the ones involving Mom's "stalkers." Mom's first stalker, a former neighbor, followed her from the townhouse complex to rehabilitation, where he visited her once or twice. She really didn't feel up to having visitors, except for family, and complained about not wanting him to visit again. I didn't know who told Ray she was there. Ray then learned that we were moving to The Terrace. On Valentine's Day, with Mom in physical therapy for an hour, my quiet writing time was interrupted with a knock on the door. One of the first responders stood at the door with Ray, who held a gold bag of chocolate peanuts. Never mind that the staff wasn't supposed to allow people who didn't know a resident's apartment number inside the gated complex, let alone lead them to the actual apartment. After uncomfortably reminding the responder of this policy and telling Ray that I didn't know when Mom would return, I took the gift and said good-bye to Mom's unwanted visitor.

A few months later, Mom's young and attractive appearance caught the eye of a resident. Ted was difficult to miss, with his long-sleeved business shirts and ties in the middle of summer. Mom mentioned him coming up to her a few times when I wasn't around as I often waited until the last minute to walk into the dining room. I didn't think anything of it until she said he grabbed her arm one day to prevent her from leaving. That worried me, and I tried to accompany Mom from then on whenever she walked anywhere. At lunch, I watched him out of the corner of my eye. We often waited until Ted left before we walked to our apartment.

One day, though, he stood outside the dining room and called Mom over to talk to him. As she said we needed to go home and we continued walking, Ted began following us! Even in both of our conditions, Mom and I outpaced him. I opened the keyless electronic lock on our door, let Mom in, and waited a few minutes.

"Mom, I'm going to the office. I'll be back soon."

My mom had lost the ability to stand up for herself. I now had to stand up for both of us. As I approached the receptionist, I saw him sitting in the waiting area. With my back to him and as quietly as possible, I told her Mom was being harassed by a resident. When she asked me if I knew the resident's name, I looked over my shoulder. She sensed that I didn't want to say anything more there, and said she would send someone up to our apartment.

A little while later, Mom and I were speaking to the new executive director and one of the first responders. I gave them more details, and they went to speak to the old coot.

Ted, the resident with the vampire-like eyes (as Mom described him), never bothered her again.

***

While Mom seemed to grudgingly adjust to our new home, I continued to have difficulties. We both needed more room, and I needed my computer in a private place. Although I continued to write online articles in the middle of our living room, often with the TV on, I yearned for my own space again. I became especially angry when Mom looked over my shoulder and read my outgoing email to family and friends. Many times, I wrote about her condition and my difficulties helping her. I tried to choose my words as carefully as possible, but I told the truth.

On a particularly horrible day, Mom and I went to the doctor to have my paratransit application renewed. We met our new physician since Dr. Ericson retired. I wanted Mom to go to the office with me. Once we arrived by shuttle, I asked Mom to take a seat in the waiting room, then I went into the examining room alone.

The doctor came in and greeted me. After greeting her, I showed her my application and explained my need for her to answer the few questions about my disability and why I couldn't use the regular bus system.

She read it for a couple of minutes and said, "I can't do this."

"What do you mean?"

"I have only met you once and I don't know enough about your disability. You need a neurologist to complete this paperwork."

"Doctor, you know that I have cerebral palsy. I haven't seen a neurologist in years. I don't have one and don't have time to go to one. I have two weeks to mail this, and I need you to fill it out."

"That's not my fault. I'm an internist, not a neurologist."

I started to go to the door to leave. The physician stopped me.

"I want my mom to come in here."

After a few minutes, Mom rolled her walker in the room. I quickly told her what was happening. My mom continued the same discussion with the doctor I started, though Mom was a little more adamant. I was proud of her.

The physician reluctantly completed the application, asking me questions about how far I could walk. She then said something that stunned my mom and me.

"I don't want to see either one of you again."

"Don't worry, we won't be back," I replied.

I still felt upset when we returned to The Terrace. After I accompanied Mom back to the apartment, I decided to go check the mail. Mom didn't want to go with me, but I needed to take a walk. I usually asked my caregiver to do this on the days she came since opening the mailbox with a key was extremely difficult for me. Sometimes, someone around the mailboxes offered to help me, or I simply took my time and struggled until I opened the slot.

Approaching the covered mailbox area, I saw a group of people talking with one another after they had picked up their mail. The mailboxes were a popular meeting place at The Terrace, and it meant I had an audience as I struggled to collect our mail. As I still felt angry and shaky from the experience at the doctor's office, my hand flailed uncontrollable as I tried to aim the key toward the lock.

"Why do they send that girl down here to get the mail? She can't do it."

I didn't need to turn around to know who made the comment. The man in the scooter continued to look in my direction. Although I knew he had some form of dementia, his words hurt and unleashed my emotions. I stood against the wall beside the mail slots and began crying. In between my tears, I tried to give him a message, though I knew he wouldn't understand me.

"I'm not deaf, and if you don't want to watch me struggle, don't look at me."

Jim, who sat at our lunch table, walked over to me. He tried to comfort me and offered to open the box for me. I tried to tell him I was having a horrible day. He didn't understand me very well, and I didn't want to stand there any longer than necessary.

"Thanks, Jim, but I want to do it myself. Please just leave me alone."

Several minutes later, I finally opened the mailbox and emptied its contents. I put our important mail on a nearby covered trash can and sorted through the junk mail. I closed the box, turned the key, and pulled it out. Picking up the mail and gripping it tightly, I managed to smile slightly at Jim as I turned to walk home.

Breaking down again in the apartment and telling Mom what happened, I announced what I had just decided.

"I can't live here any longer."

Mom and I had been discussing, and arguing about, moving. She wanted to return to our townhouse, which was now on the market. I knew that wasn't possible, but I also knew I couldn't last at The Terrace much longer. We began talking about other options, and I started picking up real estate magazines at the grocery store. Looking for two-bedroom, first floor apartments or townhomes sounded easy. Since neither one of us could drive, location held the utmost importance because we would need to rely on friends and paratransit to take us to the store and on other errands.

Cris and Chad repeatedly reminded me about the conveniences and accessibility we would abandon. I didn't need to be reminded and worried about all of the considerations that we needed to work out to make the move. I certainly understood the difficulties both Mom and I faced living somewhere else. If I continued helping Mom as much as I did each day, though, I needed more space – and a more diversified community.

Remembering a new complex of lofts that were recently built near our townhouse, I began investigating rental fees for a two-bedroom. Arnold took us to see the complex, and we loved it. Soon after our first visit, my sister saw the loft. Cris admitted that we could make it work. Almost nine months after we had moved into The Terrace, Mom and I were moving into a much more spacious home. The "adventure" was over, but as much as I wanted the loft to work out for us, something inside of me knew it wouldn't.

***

The loft gave both of us personal space. Having my own bedroom and bathroom allowed me to periodically escape from what I witnessed daily - Mom needed more and more assistance. Although I had private, quiet space again to work on my computer, I often felt too tired and too overwhelmed to write. The assistance I received from my caregiver didn't do enough to help me help Mom.

During the months leading up to the move, Mom and I discussed my decision to go to San Antonio – by myself. Laurie and I talked about my coming to Thanksgiving for months. After picking his daughter up from Santa Fe, Texas, Laurie's brother, Danny, would pick me up on his way to The Alamo City. Mom and I kept rehashing my plans to do something new - go on a solo trip. She continued asking how I would manage taking care of myself, as if I hadn't been doing that for months with minimal assistance. I kept reminding her I was going to be with family and that they would help me when I needed it.

I thought my trip would do all of us some good. Mom would stay with Cris and Chad while I was gone. I wanted my sister to realize how difficult caring for Mom each and every day had become.

After spending five days with Laurie and her husband, Joey, their son drove me home. We were running late, so I called Mom and reminded her to have my caregiver stay so she could help me when I arrived home. I wanted my caregiver to help me unpack and assist both of us with dinner. When I arrived at the loft, however, Mom had allowed the caregiver to go home. My shock back to reality jolted my entire being as I watched Mom do her best to make an easy dinner. In the days since I saw her, Mom became incredibly weaker and looked shockingly frail.

"Your sister did everything for me while I stayed with her."

"That's great, Mom. Cris doesn't live here, though. Now you can understand why I wanted my caregiver here this afternoon."

The relaxation I felt during my trip quickly disappeared.

***

The next morning, I got up for a few minutes before going back to bed to watch the news. My bedroom offered a clear view of Mom's bathroom, situated across the living room. I kept noticing the closed door with the light shining beneath it. Knowing Mom now took longer in the bathroom, I didn't think anything of it at first. After ten minutes, I began to worry and walked across the loft to check on her. I heard Mom's faint voice after knocking on the door and calling her. As I opened the door, I saw her frail body lying in front of the commode.

"Mom! How long have you been on the floor?"

"Just a little while. I tried to call you. I'm okay; I just can't get up."

210

"I'm calling 911."

Actually, I called Arnold first. I needed his calm presence with me, and I knew he would come quickly. Then I called the paramedics. Immediately, I worried that the dispatcher would have difficulty understanding my speech. She didn't, but she began asking me to check Mom's airway and to perform other measures I couldn't do.

"I have a physical disability and can't do that. My mom is breathing and appears to be okay. I just need someone to pick her up."

Trying to control my overwhelming anxiety, I hung up the phone and then called Cris.

The paramedics arrived first and helped Mom up off the floor. They asked her to walk around the living room with her walker. The men made sure Mom was safely on the couch, and confirmed that family was on the way before leaving.

What followed after Cris and Arnold arrived was a discussion among the four of us that would significantly alter my independence, and Mom's life.

***

Mom's fall before Thanksgiving 2010 resulted in significant changes in both of our lives. Just over a year later, her physical weakness and motor processing difficulties resulted in another hospital stay – followed by more rehabilitation. In January, Mom moved yet again. This time, however, I did not move with her.

Laurie rescued me again with her company and guidance. Less than twenty-four hours after I left her house in San Antonio, I called my cousin again to tell her of Mom's fall. She and I kept in close contact over the next few days. By Friday, Laurie decided to come and spend a long weekend with me. During her visits to Houston the previous year, she assisted me in packing to move from the townhouse. On this visit, Laurie guided me in making an important decision that would affect my immediate future and would begin my new life.

15
A New Life:
Remembering the Past,
Envisioning a Future

At the end of December 2011, I moved back to the third zip code (all within miles of each other) I had lived in during the past eleven months. I looked forward to leaving the loft, where I truly felt alone because of not knowing anyone in the complex - in addition to missing Mom. While I briefly considered moving to an apartment complex for individuals with disabilities, or residing closer to my sister, I made the decision that seemed the most logical and felt the most comfortable. I returned to our townhouse. The fact that the townhouse didn't sell in the six months we had it on the market seemed as if fate wanted me to come home.

Before confirming my decision, Laurie and I went out to dinner with Judy and Arnold. I asked them if they supported my choice and if they would be willing to provide assistance when I needed it. My beloved neighbors, whom I now think of as surrogate parents, welcomed me back home.

This townhouse brings back so many memories, yet holds new promise. I began a new existence, actually a new life, here. One that I didn't think I could have, or even would have wanted.

Beyond my excitement, though, realization crept into my mind that I probably would never live with Mom again. Many questions continued to enter my overwhelmed mind. Would living in the townhouse constantly remind me of Mom? How would I cope with loneliness after sharing a home for so long? At thirty-eight years old, after a few weeks of practice here and there, did I have the physical and emotional abilities to handle living independently – or at least semi-independently? Most perplexing of all, how would I create my own, meaningful life when I often wanted life before Mom's stroke, and Mom herself, back?

The townhouse looks different from the home Mom and I once shared. With improvements made before putting it on the market, and the opportunity to slowly replace the furniture Mom needed, it is now my home. Still, I remember when the two of us shared our lives here. I find myself arranging pillows on my couch the way she used to do, and doing a hundred other little tasks that I watched Mom do. Seeing an older woman walk her Bichon Frise every day through the kitchen shutters reminds me of Mom's daily routines. I can't help but wish through teary eyes that the woman was my mom. The other day, my new next-door neighbor planted flowers on both sides of my front walkway in Mom's favorite white pots, which remained empty for months. Now, when I open the kitchen shutters in the morning, the vibrant colors cheer me up.

Three weeks after I returned home, Cris moved Mom into a retirement community, a nursing home, with various levels of care. Her assisted living apartment had the look and feel of a small loft with a living room and bedroom. Mom seemed to be doing her best to adjust to a new environment, a new routine, and many new individuals taking care of her. For the first few months, I experienced immense guilt and sorrow, wondering whether I made the correct decision of living on my own. While my heart often told me otherwise, my mind knew I had chosen the best for both of us. At sixty-eight, Mom's continuous decline, with numerous falls, concentration difficulties, and frailty, confirmed her need for continuous care.

This spring, Cris brought Mom to the townhouse after we went out to lunch. I quietly watched as Mom slowly walked around downstairs and noticed the new kitchen countertops and the new carpet she will not have a chance to enjoy. I pondered what she was thinking as she remembered our days together, and realized we had to now live separately. Instead of kissing Mom goodbye before Cris walked with her out to the car, I shouted 'bye' from the bathroom. With the door closed and the faucet running, I hope she didn't hear me crying. Over the next few days, I wondered if bringing her to the townhouse was too much for her, as it was for me.

"Maybe seeing you at home will provide her some comfort and let her know you're doing okay," Arnold wisely said to me.

I hope so. I'm slowly becoming okay.

***

My caregiver situation has settled into a dependable and comfortable routine. In the beginning months of my new life, a caregiver came on weekdays in a spilt shift to make my breakfast and lunch. She then came back in the afternoon to bathe me, do household chores and prepare dinner. I still rely on that schedule twice a week. On other weekdays and weekends, my provider comes in the afternoon and prepares dinner and meals for the next day, leaving me drinks in covered cups with breakfast and lunch that I can handle independently. My coordination has improved and I don't have as many spills as I used to have. When I do create a mess, I no longer become upset or dwell on it. I simply clean up what I can and go on with the rest of the day. If I want or need to go somewhere, I take MetroLift or ask Arnold if it is convenient for him to drive me. Sometimes, I meet my caregiver at my destination, or we go together.

I regularly visit the places Mom and I used to go to together. The first few weeks of running errands, or going to the store or to the pharmacy, people who always saw the two of us continually asked, "Where's your mom?." As touched as I was (and still am) with their care and concern, that frequent question reminded me of the many changes and losses in our lives. Telling better-known acquaintances and friends about the past two years remains especially difficult; the more they know Mom, the better they understand how much her life – and mine - have changed. I receive comfort for both of us, particularly for Mom, whose loses and disabilities are far greater than mine.

I try to pass that comfort to Mom each week I visit her. Although I usually go every Saturday, I visited her one weekday this summer. That afternoon, she happened to have PT and OT. Sitting on her couch while the therapists worked with her, I thought about Mom watching me, all those years ago, following the physical therapist's instructions and trying to make my muscles cooperate with exercises they sometimes didn't want to do. Observing her attempts to perform tasks she once did easily, I identified with the sadness, frustration, and worry Mom must have felt during my childhood. Only as I grew, and continue growing, into the reversed role of a daughter with special needs, whose mother now has special needs, did I truly understand these emotions about a loved one with a disability.

Barely eight months after her move into assisted living, Mom fell again and broke her right elbow and wrist. After having multiple surgeries on her elbow, she returned to the same facility. This time, she was placed in skilled nursing. Cris and I are hoping Mom will be able to soon return to her assisted living apartment. I don't know if that will be possible.

In between my Saturday visits with Mom, I continue to work on creating my own, meaningful life. Writing this book represented an important and necessary step in the journey to achieving this goal. I needed to look back at the many experiences which brought me where I am today before thinking about tomorrow. If anything I have written makes some aspect of anyone's life, with or without a disability, a little easier, or allows someone to feel less alone, then I will consider my efforts in writing this book extremely meaningful.

I realize how fortunate I am to have the community supports I need to live by myself. Not everyone with disabilities has them. This reality is one of the main reasons I experienced so much anxiety as I reached adulthood. I didn't understand how I could possibly live on my own without Mom's physical presence and assistance. Aside from our occasional discussions about what my life could possibly look like "when Mom was no longer here," an independent life remained an unimaginable and frightening mystery. I did not realize the great realities and opportunities of this new and different life until I tried living independently.

Community living and other issues involving people with disabilities are now in the news more than ever. As I write this in October 2012, the federal government has again proclaimed this month as National Disability Employment Awareness Month. The high unemployment rate of individuals with disabilities has been a national focus this year. Still, this issue, along with other practical, real issues of living with a disability, overlooked or continually unmet, continue to pose significant challenges to the majority of us. Until everyone has increased access to opportunities, though, many lives, including mine, will remain preoccupied with creating meaningful ways to fulfill our potential.

Throughout my search, I will stay determined in keeping my balance.

Epilogue

A week from today will be Thanksgiving 2012. Like last Thanksgiving, I will celebrate with my family in San Antonio. This year, however, I will fly by myself to visit Laurie and my other cousins. My trip will be the second time I will travel independently. Last June, I took the short flight to spend a week with my beloved cousin. I would be lying if I didn't admit to feeling slightly nervous. Slightly, though, because my excitement seemed to outweigh my anxiety. The many personnel who assisted me in the airport allowed me to experience life as an independent traveler, with one airline employee telling me, "We're glad we could give you some new-found independence."

I've actually experienced many firsts this year. I recently voted in person for the first time, discarding my absentee ballot. After a few minor difficulties giving my name and asking the poll workers to speak directly to me, rather than to my caregiver, I operated the machine myself. A week later, I opened my own bank account, with Arnold quietly observing as I discussed options with the banker. I've also continued to handle most of my personal business, and much of Mom's, making my own phone calls and settling matters that involve both of our futures.

Celebrating these small successes helps me in maintaining somewhat of an emotional balance as Cris and I deal with Mom's declining health. Two weeks ago, the decision was made to keep Mom in skilled nursing. The decision didn't surprise me, but as Cris brought many of Mom's belongings to the townhouse, I felt the continuing loss we have experienced during the past two difficult years. The day after tomorrow, I will visit Mom again, spending a Saturday with her that doesn't much remind me of past Saturdays we spent together. I don't need reminding, though. Mom always said I have an excellent memory.

Acknowledgements

I owe many people my unending gratitude for supporting the writing of my book. For years, Mom encouraged me to begin a memoir and avoid worrying about how long I took to complete it. Although we lived apart when I finally embarked on this endeavor, I felt her love and presence as I wrote each page. My independence, my determination, and my story, would not exist without her.

Laura Mendez, my cousin, read the rough, rough draft and believed I created publishable material from the beginning. Her encouragement, editing, and feedback kept me writing and wanting to improve the telling of my experiences.

Dr. Nancy Russell insisted that I include everything I needed to put into words, and gave me wonderful suggestions along the way. She read the manuscript early in the editing process.

Judy and Arnold Dewey define the meaning of neighbors and "adoptive" parents. Their love and dedication helped me survive many difficulties and create an independent life. I appreciate their encouragement to join a writer's group, and the rides to share my work. Betsy Dewey, my "sister-in-law," read my work and offered valuable advice on promoting the book – and myself. I thank her for giving me a stronger voice on the Internet.

Jeff Payne, Robin Payne, and the team at AscendWorks presented me with a wonderful website and beautiful book cover. I'm grateful for all of their talent and generosity.

Finally, I'd like to thank the Houston Writers Guild, particularly Lynne Gregg, Roger Paulding, Sandra DiGiovanni, and Lilia Fabry. Lynne welcomed me into her home and into her heart, and provided final editing before I attended my first writing conference. Roger's comments made me feel like a professional, and Sandra encouraged me to include the beginning of my story in "OMG – That Woman!" Lilia revealed it online. The four of them, along with all of my HWG friends, liven up my Saturday mornings.

Share your thoughts about "Keeping My Balance: A Memoir of Disability and Determination." As an indie author, I would appreciate your honest review of my memoir. Please post your comments on Amazon.com. Thank you!

CPSIA information can be obtained
at www.ICGtesting.com
Printed in the USA
LVHW042122151220
674262LV00012B/1046